THE LAUGH AND THE TEARS

Building A Jewish School To
Reveal The 'Kisharon' Of Each Child

by
Chava Lehman

Mazo Publishers
Jerusalem, Israel

THE LAUGHTER AND THE TEARS
ISBN: 978-965-7344-72-9
Copyright © 2011 Chava Lehman

Contact the Author:
Email: cmml@netvision.net.il

Published by:
Mazo Publishers
Chaim Mazo, Publisher
P.O. Box 36084
Jerusalem 91360 Israel

Website: www.mazopublishers.com
Email: cm@mazopublishers.com
Israel: 054-7294-565
USA: 1-815-301-3559

All rights reserved.
No part of this publication may be translated, reproduced, stored in a retrieval system, or transmitted in any form or by any means, electronic, mechanical, photocopying, recording or otherwise, without prior permission in writing from the publisher.

In Memory Of

Moshe and Clara Robinson – my parents
Meir Robinson – my brother
Pat Hoddes – my cousin
Zoe Jacobs – my great niece

And my friends

Lady J
Walter Bentley
Pamela Kersh
Elisheva Lebrett
Judy Price
Janet Shine
Hinda Stile

'Kisharon'

A Hebrew word meaning skill, talent or flair.

'We knew what things the children found so difficult – but it was our aim to discover the Kisharon in each child'.

Contents

Humpty Dumpty	8
Preface	11
Introduction	15

Part One
Pioneering Kisharon   19

A Need In Jewish Education	21
Early Days In The Back Office	26
Getting Started	28
The Nursery And The Babies	35
Chanela	37

Part Two
Activities and Curriculum   39

School Ethos	41
Getting Out And About	43
Music	48
Sit Like A 'Mensh'	48
The Rings	51
Friday Discussion Group	52
Oneg Shabbat	53
Shabbaton	56
Bar Mitzvah And Sheva Brachot Celebrations	60

Part Three
The Kisharon Heroes   63

Parents Are Our Partners	65
1011 Finchley Road	67
Medical Matters	73
Asperger's Syndrome	76
Speechmaking	78
Her Majesty's Inspector – Kathy Bull	80
Birth Of Senior Centre One: The Coach House	81
The Hanna Schwalbe Home	85
Skeet House	88
Last Day At Skeet	95
Off To Israel – 1991	97
Finance	101
The Volunteers	104
The Unsung Heroes	105
North London Friends Of Kisharon	108
Roll Of Honour	109

Part Four
And They Grow Up   111

Tefillah Lechol Yisrael	113
And The Tears...	117
Acknowledgments	121

Humpty Dumpty

Humpty Dumpty went to a school
He could not keep up, so they called him a fool
They kept him in class with very bad grace
Because he could not keep up with the learning race.

Humpty Dumpty wanted to learn
The smiles of his teacher he wanted to earn
But he found it so hard to concentrate
When the learning went at such a fast rate.

Say it together, again and again
He tried with all his might and main
He squirmed in his seat, as the lesson droned on
He wished he could jump and run in the sun.

If only someone would stop and explain
If only someone would ease his pain
At being the one who couldn't cope
Of gradually giving up all hope.

Humpty Dumpty grew very sad
They said his behaviour was very bad
He was NEVER given a chance to excel
At the tasks he COULD DO exceedingly well.

Humpty Dumpty joined a new school
Where respect for each pupil was the rule
He began to learn at his very own pace
He was finally out of the learning race.

Now Humpty Dumpty enjoys going to school
He's too busy learning to play the fool
He studies with all his might and main
Humpty Dumpty is together again.

Preface

This work was written without the benefit of notes or diaries and written following our *Aliyah* (Emigration) to Israel in 2006. I have simply recorded my recollections of how life was for those of us who were privileged to work in and for Kisharon from 1976 until my retirement in 2002.

Some wonderful people helped us over the years; some are mentioned in the book – others are not, for this story is mainly about the children. For all of us, they came first. Most names have been changed to ensure privacy and I feel certain that I have muddled some of the dates – setting the story down on paper seemed more important than time-consuming checking of records.

Some remarkable people joined our team and, to this day, we share a wonderful bond and many precious and privileged memories. In sharing my memories, I wish to honour the committee, the staff and all the volunteers who worked so devotedly for Kisharon; and also my family, without whose support I could never have given the necessary time to getting the school up and running, thriving and developing: my husband, Manny, who was also a hardworking member of the committee; and our children. Their unstinting support and

Manny Lehman speaks at the opening of 1011 Finchley Road.

loving-kindness is what kept (and keeps!) me going.

Many of these chapters were written while waiting in line for a unique doctor, Dr Hadassah Greidinger of Jerusalem. No '7 minutes' for her! She gives you all the time you need, calmly and cheerfully. Consequently, of course, there is often a long queue outside her door, but the time I spent there passed in a flash as I scribbled away, reliving our days in Kisharon.

My thanks to Hinda Style, who turned the scribbling into well-typed sheets – and to her grandchildren who taught her how to send attachments.

When Cecily Davis, my then secretary, co-founder and close friend, read the first proof of this book, she said, 'You must write about the children', so, as ever, I am taking her advice and this narrative will be spiced with true stories of children who found their 'Kisharon' in our school. This is also a good opportunity to thank Cecily for her tremendous support

Preface

in getting Kisharon up and running and in ensuring its high reputation in the community.

I have used many Hebrew terms and Jewish concepts throughout the text which might make the book less comprehensible to readers without the relevant background. Since the essence of Kisharon was that the richness of Jewish Custom should be available to all members of the Jewish Faith – even those who are less able – it would not be in that spirit to secularize the story. Nevertheless the story of Kisharon and its message is universal and needs to be told to a wider audience. Since I find in-line translation disturbing, I have added footnotes that not only translate the terms but also give some of the background.

If this book appears light-hearted, it is because that is how I recall those times. Yes, we had terrible days when some pupils just couldn't settle down and we were at our wits' end. But that is what we were there for, that was the challenge – it was part of our job and as such blended into the background. As one member of the staff put it to a new colleague, 'If you can't look after and teach these children with love and patience, then you should be stacking shelves in a supermarket'.

Introduction

I trained to be a teacher at Sunderland Training College, a department of Durham University. In my first year as a teacher and still under supervision, I was sent to work in a small school in the poorest district of a northern English town.

It was mid-winter of 1952. The area was under deep snow with coal fires the only form of heating. I taught a class of six-year-olds – forty boys and girls from poor homes, mainly children of miners, and many of them inadequately dressed for the freezing weather.

David, a thin, undersized little boy with a permanently running nose, wore ill-fitting shoes, short trousers and no socks, topped by an ancient, filthy coat with no buttons. He shook with cold and one day I said to him, 'Ask your mother to sew some buttons on your coat, David, then you'll be warmer'. He nodded shyly. Next day I waited for him to come cosily buttoned up in his coat, which he always wore indoors.

In he came, pale and shivering. 'Me Ma says she got no buttons'.

'Don't worry', I said, 'I'll find some buttons for you'. During my lunch break I went to Woolworth and bought six large navy buttons and sent them home with the little boy after school. Next day David came in and handed me back the packet of buttons.

'Me Ma says, if it bothers you, Miss, *you* stitch them on'. Of course I did. Many years later, married and the mother of five children, having returned to teaching after a hiatus of fifteen years, I remembered David and his buttonless coat. With hindsight, I believe that this event triggered my interest in children who, for one reason or another, were disadvantaged or who needed moral support as well as teaching.

During the year I spent at this school, I was knocked into shape by Miss Brydon, the headmistress. She would sail into the room unannounced, open all the cupboards and begin counting. Today children hump everything they need for the day on their backs, but in 1952 schools provided everything. Forty children equaled forty pencils, forty tins of crayons (broken and smelly!), forty tins of plasticine and so on. If just one thing was missing or a puzzle incomplete, she would order me, 'Stay behind until everything is found'.

I learnt to collect empty tins from peas and fruit, clean them, cover them and store the equipment. I learnt to make what was then called 'apparatus': forty individual cards, each with a picture on top and questions about the picture underneath. No workbooks for us, no photocopied worksheets. The corners of those cards had to be cut into half-circles and the whole lot varnished! Everything we used was handmade in our own time. The expression 'non-teaching time' was only introduced many years later.

Being young and enthusiastic and with art as one of my main subjects at college, I had no problem with all this and was happy enough in my work until the day Miss Brydon breezed in and in her usual no-nonsense way said, 'It's now November. I'm not interested that you're Jewish. You have to produce a nativity play with your class'. Fortunately, I had attended a non-Jewish school (though I regret not having had the privilege of going to a Jewish school) and had stood at the back of the room during all the pre-Xmas preparations and carol-singing. I knew the whole procedure backwards but, of course, had never participated. I did as Miss Brydon said, for I had no option.

Later she had the grace to say, 'Well, your play was the best'!

Many years later I was speaking at a prize day at the Hasmonean Girls School in London. Our granddaughter was head girl and she had primed me, 'Keep it light, be funny, we're fed up with serious stuff all the time'.

I stood in front of four hundred girls who had never in their lives attended non-Jewish schools and would be horrified at the mere thought. I asked them, 'How many of you know what a nativity play is'? About four hands crept slowly up. I then told them the story of my experiences as a trainee teacher in a non-Jewish environment, about David and his buttons and about the nativity play I had to produce. There was dead silence as I urged them to appreciate their Jewish education, not to take it for granted and to give thought to the future when so many qualified teachers would be needed for the ever-growing number of Jewish schools around the world.

My words shocked the girls out of their complacency and gave them food for thought. And obviously, my failure to comply with my granddaughter's request to 'be funny' had no lasting effect on her: she is now a qualified teacher of both secular subjects and Hebrew Studies and the mother of three children.

These pages are not only a history of a school, but also of a new awakening in the Jewish community. Children who for one reason or another did not glide through the natural milestones of development suddenly became a factor to be reckoned with. No hiding the problems away, but rather looking for new solutions and finding them in most innovative ways. The community is learning to love and understand the children and to include them in various activities.

Certainly, the most important development has been the special programmes that followed in the footsteps of Kisharon and, as I write in 2008, parents have stepped into lead positions, providing help, support and exciting activities for both children and parents.

G-d sends us thousands of beautiful healthy children who follow the natural milestones of development with ease. We often take this for granted. We thank Him but we should also pray that He will grant us the knowledge, patience and love to help those whose development does not proceed quite so smoothly, but who have amazing potential if given the right encouragement and care.

However, raising a child who is different remains a source of distress and a challenge. Now at least, thanks to new knowledge and expertise in the Jewish community, help is at hand, provision is growing and the community is waking up to the fact that life is for everyone, even for those who need help to live it to the fullest.

Part One
Pioneering Kisharon

A Need In Jewish Education

The traffic is always dreadful in London's Finchley Road, but never more so than on the day I had an appointment with Amelie, the wife of the Chief Rabbi, HaRav Lord Jakobovits. Once, when I was telling this story in public, I added, 'But she wasn't a *Lady* then'. It got a huge laugh at the time, but Lady J, as she is now fondly known, had no need of her husband's honour to be a lady. She was a lady in her own right.

Shy by nature even today, I was certainly worse in 1975 when I was the remedial teacher (now called SENCO) at one of the local Jewish schools, having returned to teaching after a fifteen-year gap. When the traffic had at last edged its way through Swiss Cottage and deposited me at 85 Hamilton Terrace, I rang the bell, determined to share my concerns about underachieving children. I was warmly welcomed into a small cosy seating area, given a hot drink and encouraged to tell my story.

I told Lady Jakobovits about the plight of children in Jewish schools who were not coping, children who needed specialised teaching in small groups to enable them to overcome their learning disabilities. Totally absorbed in what

I had to say (concern with everyone's celebrations, problems and sorrows is, of course, Lady J's hallmark), she promised to speak to the Chief Rabbi and ushered me out saying, 'Someone has to work on it day and night, every Jewish child must be offered an education'.

At the bus stop, feeling encouraged by Lady J's sympathy and interest, I nominated myself, at the very least, to get things moving. Following endless discussions with my husband, children and professionals in the field of special education and a further meeting with the late Moshe Davis, the Chief Rabbi authorised his office to provide £5,000 seed money towards the establishment of a special school. There were two conditions: an initial enrolment of at least three children and the formation of a management committee. My husband scouted around for suitable candidates to be on the committee. The first meeting was held in the home of Max Sulzbacher. Max was our first chairman and worked with enthusiasm. Mrs Sulzbacher sent us wonderful fruit baskets each holiday.

Throughout the following years, as Kisharon grew and developed, the Chief Rabbi and Lady Jakobovits strengthened our resolve with friendly phone calls and were guests of honour as we opened each new building.

I placed a letter in the Jewish Chronicle and three intrepid parents came forward. They are the real pioneers of Kisharon. In 1975, children with severe or even mild learning difficulties had either to go to non-Jewish schools or to stay at home. The whole subject tended to be swept under the carpet, although there were wonderful families, even then, who faced the problem bravely and encouraged their children to be, as much as possible, part of the social scene.

Initially we rented three rooms in Finchley Road, London,

NW11, and I began interviewing the children. I said to one little boy who was attending a non-Jewish school, 'This is a new school and I'm buying everything we're going to need. Is there any special game or toy you'd like'? He thought for just a few seconds before replying, 'I only want *one thing*, kosher lunches'! This summed up how a child might feel going to a school where he could not fully belong.

It is often said that by opening Kisharon we opened the doors (and eyes and hearts) to a common problem and led the way by fostering communal awareness of very personal and often tragic problems. With awareness came interest; and with interest and goodwill, there sprang up various sources of help for children who had previously floundered in the back row or wandered the corridors!

My husband, Manny, supported and encouraged me from the beginning. Our five children, then aged between six and twenty, always came first and the youngest became a dab hand at answering the phone with, 'Please would you ring my Mummy after eight'.

An insomniac for as long as I can remember, I tried to ensure that most of the written work and phone calls necessary to get the school off the ground were done at night after the younger children had been put to bed. Nevertheless, the children must have felt the pressure and that was their (hopefully willing) contribution, for they never complained.

I visited many special education schools seeking advice and ideas for; after all, we were sailing in uncharted waters. One head teacher told me, 'We do our best for our Jewish children, but one little girl is so distressed when she sees the lovely desserts which she's not allowed to eat, that we have to give it to her too'.

It is indeed hard for any Jewish child to attend a secular school and be 'different'. He or she cannot eat lunch with the other children, cannot participate in holiday celebrations and, above all, cannot talk about and share the Jewish way of life. Early Fridays can be a nightmare for a sensitive child in an uncooperative school, how much more so for a child with limited speech and communication problems. Even today I am sad when I hear that a child has to attend a non-Jewish school in order to receive specialised help, and I know that the parents and siblings suffer along with the child.

Children who cannot keep up in class either withdraw into themselves or resort to poor or even challenging behaviour. Over the years, as a remedial teacher as it was then called, I met children whose poor behaviour inhibited their learning – and standing in the corridor did nothing to improve their attitude! All it did was to make the child miss lessons, get farther and farther behind; the net result: even worse behaviour and frustration all round.

One of our first pupils, a six-year-old, had been excluded from several schools before arriving on our doorstep. In desperation, his mother begged us to accept him. He was articulate and bright, but capable of wrecking a room, kicking, biting and hurling into the air anything not nailed down. At that time we had a rather fierce caretaker with a strong Yorkshire accent. One day, when all else had failed and we were desperate, I told the caretaker that the next time Lenny wrecked the room he was to come in and act very angry (in 1976 we were not scared of a bit of old-fashioned discipline). It did not take long for the room to be wrecked and, as planned, in walked Mr Humphrey, hands on hips, eyes glaring. In his broadest accent he declared, 'You wreck mah room and Ah'll be after you'! At that moment, Lenny, having swept everything off the shelves, was lying stretched out on the top shelf. He sat up, visibly paled, hesitated a moment and climbed down. Mr Humphrey stood over him until every single thing was back in place.

After this, I only had to announce, 'I'm calling Mr Humphrey'! and Lenny calmed down. It didn't happen in a week or even a month but slowly, as his behaviour improved, his schoolwork sank in and his efforts started to bear fruit, his attitude became more positive until one day he said to me, 'I really don't belong here. Can I go to a regular school'? It took approximately two years for him to be totally integrated back into mainstream education. Many times I would ring him in the evening and say, 'Lenny, I can't have a day like this again. What will tomorrow be like'? After a moment's silence I would hear a chuckle and the soft reply, 'I'll be good – I promise', and he was. During really bad patches, his wonderful mother would sit in the school, 'just in case', and that got us through some difficult days.

One day he came to school looking rather pale. 'Can I speak to you privately'? he whispered. 'Of course', I said, ushering him into my office.

'Last night', he began slowly, looking down at the floor, 'My Dad took me down to the police station, threw me at the front desk and told the policeman on duty, 'I want you to lock him up and show him where his bad behaviour will lead him'.'

'What happened then', I asked, thinking it was another of his stories.

'I asked for a kosher meal and a TV in my cell'! he said proudly. I calmed him down and he went back to class. Half an hour later the phone rang. It was Lenny's mother. She sounded distraught.

'You won't believe this, Mrs Lehman, but last night my husband was furious with Lenny. He put him in the car, drove to the police station' ... and she repeated Lenny's story word for word. 'Is he all right'? she ended up.

I reassured her but didn't divulge the fact that I had already heard the story. Many years later, there was a knock at the door and a tall, handsome young man stood there.

'Don't you remember me'? he asked. It was Lenny.

I showed him round our beautiful new building and, as he left, he put his arm round me, handed me an envelope and said, 'You're doing a great job'! I slid into my chair, visibly moved, and slowly opened the envelope. Inside was a cheque for £1,000 made out to *Kisharon Day School*.

Early Days In The Back Office

Our first building was an old-fashioned house with a small 'morning room' which became my office and a 'scullery' which came to be known as the 'back office'.

There was a bell in each classroom and when a teacher 'pushed the button' a light flashed on a panel in my office showing in which room I was needed in the event that a child was having a convulsion or misbehaving or if any other incident required an extra pair of hands. One of the pupils once asked me, 'Mrs Lehman, what if the emergency is in your room'?

That only happened once in 26 years – a parent really 'lost it' and screamed at me. I sat quietly with arms folded, saying nothing until she calmed down. A week later she appeared on my doorstep with a gorgeous bunch of flowers – no words were needed.

My office was used if a child was feeling ill, 'stroppy' or

generally in need of extra care. It was a part of my work that I loved. The back office, however, had its own share of action and was presided over by Cecily Davis on Mondays and Wednesdays and by her sister-in-law, Margaret Hammond, on Tuesdays and Thursdays. Friday I had to manage on my own.

Cecily Davis was school bursar and caterer of our wonderful *bar mitzvah* and *sheva brachot*[1] celebrations; but, above all, she was a wonderful sounding board for me until she retired two years before I did. After I had supervised the children's lunchtime, she and I would retreat into the back office and share cheese and mustard-pickle rolls (one and a half each) from the local bakery. (Why do so many good things disappear?!)

Cecily always gave me a lift home and on many an occasion we just sat in the car while I let off steam (or rejoiced!) over the day's events. In the back office Cecily and Margaret banged away on an old typewriter, copied things on a Banda (hand-operated copier), answered the phone and the door, made coffee and counted all the money that came in *pushkas* (charity collection boxes) and donations.

Even when a child foraging for biscuits sent everything on her desk flying or toppled her carefully sorted columns of coins, Cecily managed to stay calm. If a child was having a full-blown tantrum, she would dash in to help with the reminder, 'Take the shoes off'! It was no fun being kicked by a heavy pair of school shoes! On a few occasions (of which I am certainly not proud) the shoes went home in a plastic bag and the parents knew we had had a bad day, but I only did this after having

---

1. A bar mitzvah is a celebration when a boy reaches manhood at the age of 13. Girls celebrate a bat mitzvah at the age of 12. Sheva brachot is a festive meal in honour of a newlywed couple.

obtained parental consent and it did act as a deterrent – oh, the good old days of judiciously applied discipline!

As Head, I adopted a policy of leading from the front. I could not have done it without my wonderful secretaries over the years.

As the school grew and Margaret left, Ann Nachshon and Friedel Tiefenbrunner joined the administrative team on a part-time basis. Both Ann and Friedel were very special ladies. Sadly following grave illnesses which they battled with great fortitude, they left grieving family, friends and colleagues while still in their prime.

Our first integrated nursery, which opened in 1978, was sponsored by the Nachshon family and was named Gan Chaya in memory of Ann (Chaya). Before the onset of her illness, Friedel joined our staff as head of the nursery and she introduced us to the concept of one-to-one teaching balanced by plenty of group work. As Friedel's illness began to sap her strength, she transferred to the office and took over from Margaret. Ill though she was, her commonsense, humour and winning personality made her a valuable member of our team. We were very privileged to have had the support of these two fine ladies during our pioneering days.

Getting Started

From day one we decided to run things as professionally as possible. We registered with the Department of Education, the fire department and the police. We called the fledgling school 'Kisharon Tuition Centre' until the day in 1976 of our first inspection by HMI John Woodend.

Although totally different from the Ofsted (Office for Standards in Education) of today, it was nevertheless with some trepidation that I opened the door when the big day arrived to find a benign-looking gentleman standing on the doorstep. He introduced himself and, while still on the doorstep, said, 'Show me your fire certificate, love'.

'Fire certificate'? I echoed, somewhat amazed.

'Yes, because if you haven't got one, I can't inspect the school and you'll fail straightaway'. I rushed off to get the precious document and handed it over for his inspection. Satisfied, he took off his hat, came in and happily joined me in a cup of tea.

Mr Woodend was very satisfied with everything and had only two questions: 'Why do you call it Kisharon Tuition Centre when it's a school, and why do you call yourself Centre Supervisor'?

'Oh', I said. 'I'm only just getting it off the ground. I have no intention of being the head teacher. I have five children and a husband who often travels'.

'You're doing a splendid job', he said. 'Just go to a few courses and I'll help you all I can'.

So I did and he did: the 'Centre' became the 'Kisharon Day School' and I became a Head Teacher. Mr Woodend was true to his word and kept a fatherly eye on us. His encouragement and guidance got us off to a positive start. He would often ring up with suggestions or send photographs of suitable equipment he had seen somewhere. Unfortunately, Mr Woodend died, but subsequent inspectors were just as helpful and offered more practical help than one obtains with the current method of inspection.

So with three children in two rooms we got started. The children were taught in the morning by Bernice Berman and in the afternoon by Beryl Mosselson. The Jewish Studies or

Limudei Kodesh (LK) programme permeated everything we did. Esther Hersh was our first LK assistant. After taking time off to raise a family, she is still teaching in Kisharon and is still devoted to the young adults in her care, infusing the Jewish Studies curriculum with enthusiasm, greatly enhanced by her personal ethos and her excellent computer-generated material.

As more children joined us, they were divided into ability groups, each led by a qualified teacher. Each teacher had a *Jewish Studies* Assistant who was responsible for ensuring that the school's religious character was maintained and that it enriched the entire programme.

The inspiration for our religious ethos was provided by Rev Meir Lev (whose main job was *chazzan* (cantor) at the Golders Green Beth HaMedrash) – fondly known as 'Mister Lev'. He remained at the school until 2004 and set a unique tone of kindness, caring and the ability to enthuse the children. He used to say, 'If the child can speak, I'll teach him or her to read Hebrew' – and in many cases he did.

Mister Lev was also our willing handyman and I would greet him each day with whatever had broken since the previous day. He not only checked that the boys wore *Arba Kanfot*[2] – at times I even found him washing them if he was unhappy with their state!

But why the name 'Kisharon'? Kisharon is the Hebrew word for talent, flair, skill. Everyone has the ability to excel at something, not just the obvious subjects such as art or music, but in attributes such as friendliness, helpfulness or tidiness. It became our daily aim to help the children explore their potential, to offer them a wide variety of activities in order to

---

2. A special garment worn by religious Jews.

see which activities, given care and skilled help, they could do well and enthusiastically. At the same time, we helped them with all those tasks of daily living and learning which they found so difficult and, in so doing, we boosted their confidence and gave their parents hope, help and a sense of purpose. Best of all, the children thrived as they explored their natural talents.

In order to do this, an Individual Learning Programme (ILP) was drawn up for each child by the teacher and parents and in accordance with the child's wishes. The ILP would, for example, include the normal school subjects plus:

- dressing and undressing
- not touching displays or strangers in shops
- special exercises
- help with eating
- home behaviour

Each programme was tailor-made to the needs of the child and reviewed regularly. It was heartening to watch the children grow in confidence as they explored new subjects and were helped towards independence. The children were offered a wide range of therapies and we were very fortunate in our therapists: Helen Smuts – music therapy: Sima Berger – occupational therapy: Carmel Deutch – speech therapy. Over the years they were joined by Joy Chesterman and Ruthie Shine. They all made a great contribution to the life of the school.

I always felt that we were sailing in uncharted waters and these ladies greatly added to our professionalism, our understanding of the children and the quality of instruction.

Kisharon offered the children a spirit and atmosphere to

match their Jewish home environment. The *Limudei Kodesh* programme permeated everything we did – how we dressed, how we spoke and how we behaved to one another. *Shabbat* and *Yom Tov*[3] preparations were the highlights of the programme and helped the children feel on a level with their siblings and be in tune with family life and conversation.

Parents, and sometimes grandparents, were our partners. We spoke to them regularly and made every effort to solve school problems in school. Each day the children were sent home with a home-book and we tried very hard to make the reports as positive as possible.

Those children who had been in non-Jewish schools really thrived in the Jewish atmosphere and those who had been floundering and sometimes bullied in Jewish mainstream schools enjoyed being in an environment where whatever they could do well was appreciated and nurtured, while help was on hand for the things they found difficult.

Naturally, we became involved in home problems – behaviour, enuresis and sibling stress. Parents were positive and hardworking, but some of the children had really challenging behaviour, often the result of boredom and frustration.

Shabbat and *Yom Tov* are wonderful, but less so if you can't read a book, follow the *davening* in *shul* or go out with

---

3. Shabbat (Sabbath) – Saturday is the Jewish day of rest. Yom Tov refers to the many Jewish festivals – Rosh Hashana, Yom Kippur, Pesach, Sukkot and Shavuot. Some of the festivals are solemn, others are joyful, but all of them are quite literally a central part of religious Jewish life – not only on the festival days but also in the weeks that proceed them. The day are days of rest, of family gathering, and of course the daily prayers (*davening*) in shul, the community synagogue.

friends. As I write this, the problem remains: a problem that can only be solved by helpful friends and neighbours who will keep a child or young adult occupied or, as the children grow into adulthood and their requirements change, will meet their special needs in residential care.

Before long, the local education authority sent in their psychologists to see what we were up to. On one occasion, just before *Rosh Hashana*, an educational psychologist came to test all the children. At midmorning break he came into my tiny office (the kitchen of the house) and said, 'Mrs Lehman, something strange is going on. I point to an apple expecting the children to tell me it is a fruit and they all say the same: "You dip it in honey"'![4]

That made our day and compensated for all the aggravation, hard work and daring of putting Kisharon on the map. It proved, even to the experts, that our children needed to be in a Jewish school 'that spoke their language'. It also highlighted the urgent need for Jewish educational psychologists.

On another occasion I was allowed to watch through a two-way mirror as one of our girls was tested at the Tavistock Clinic. She was given a word and had to explain what it meant. As her first language was Yiddish, I was somewhat apprehensive, but my worry turned into delighted laughter as I heard the following:

'This is a *pahtch*. Tell me what it is'.

Chana replied without hesitation, 'Ah SMACK'![5]

---

4. It is a custom during the Jewish New Year to eat an apple dipped in honey which symbolizes the wish for a 'sweet' year.

5. Pahtch – the Yiddish word for a small 'educational' smack.

Long-standing school chairman Mr Bentley opening the new school building at 678 Finchley.

With the educational side going well and the roll growing, I was able to concentrate on getting the children from the various outlying districts to school and back home again. Our three rooms were on the busy Finchley Road and we did not have a dropped curb or driveway. Towards the end of the school day, I had to go outside and almost lie down in the road to save a parking place for the small coach. We applied to have the curb dropped but were told we would need plans, drawings and planning permission, and even then there were several other hurdles to be crossed before the curb could be dropped. Plans and drawings required money, so we struggled on until one day the pavements on Finchley Road were taken up in order to lay new gas pipes.

As the work of renewing the paving stones reached our building at 678, I sauntered over to the workmen waving a £5 note and said, 'Our minibus has a real problem parking and some of our children have difficulty walking. Do you think you could drop the curb'? Next day the minibus parked at our newly-dropped curb! I did not have to risk life and limb and, as I am known to be very law-abiding, I hope I can be forgiven for this one mild foray into bribery and corruption!

Chief Rabbi Jakobovits affixes the mezzuzah at the entrance of Kisharon.

The Nursery And The Babies

By 1979, Kisharon was becoming well-known and parents of very young children with various special needs began showing an interest in our school. So we rented the next floor, sent the 'old timers' upstairs and, under the inspired leadership of Friedel Tiefenbrunner, opened the *Gan* (nursery).

These children were much more disabled than our older children, but Friedel did a great deal of one-to-one work with them and they all made good progress. It was wonderful to see the older children help the younger ones and it was deemed a special treat to 'help' in the Gan.

Our occupational therapist, Sima Berger, had been trained at Hadassah Hospital in Israel. She felt that babies with Down's Syndrome should be given treatment as early as six weeks old, so we rented the top floor and the 'Baby Room' came into being.

It was a novel idea at the time, certainly in Jewish circles, and we owe a debt of gratitude to Sima and to those brave mothers who had to carry their babies up three flights of stairs.

The mothers loved it. Here was someone who besides treating their children, also taught them how to massage their babies with oil, how to hold them in order to strengthen their back and, perhaps just as important, how to cope with the stress of having given birth to a baby who was different and needed so much care.

New words entered our vocabulary via Sima: 'vestibular system'; 'crossing the midline'; and 'pincer grip', and new equipment was installed in the baby room. I personally learnt so much from Sima: how to show each child respect, to wonder at a baby whose elaborate faculties are all intact.

We tend to take it for granted that a baby will smile, raise its head, roll over, sit up and eventually stand and speak. These natural milestones that I had been fortunate enough to witness in our own five children suddenly took on a whole new dimension. Years later, when the grandchildren began to arrive, I was not so naive and I watched their development with new and often anxious eyes.

All the mothers used to pop in to let me cuddle their babies before they began the long climb upstairs. One in particular was particularly cute. 'Don't get too attached', warned Sima, 'It will break your heart' ... and it did when she passed away at the age of one year. I kept a large picture of her in my office and took strength from it on difficult days. Many years later one of her brothers, who had never known her as she had died before he was born, saw the picture and was gratified that his little sister had not been forgotten.

Chanela

We never thought she would sit stand or walk.

For most of her all too short life she came to us ... up the stairs with Mummy to the therapy room. Four steep flights of stairs, up up up to Sima.

All the way up, heads popped out

'Hello Chanela'!

Everyone loved her and long before she herself responded, it was worthwhile coming to say hello to her Mummy. You felt better for it, forgot your own troubles, tried a little harder...

'Hello Chanela'.

The doctors said she would never walk – her hips were too weak to carry her weight. Four flights of stairs up to Sima!

Was it worth it? Oh yes, up they went – indomitable mother and child – encouraging even Sima to keep trying.

And one day, we could not believe it – Chanela on all fours – Chanela standing and Chanela walking and climbing up, up up to Sima – Imperious call...

'Sima Sima'!

Heads popping out – 'Hello Chanela'.

We will remember Chanela.
We will remember her parents.
We will remember her long climb upwards.
We smile at the memory –
   perky tartan kilt, perky pony tail – up, up.

'Hello Chanela'.
'Sima Sima'!

Part Two
Activities and Curriculum

School Ethos

Many schools in London provide good education and care for children who are unable to benefit from mainstream education. In 1976, however, Kisharon was the only such school for Jewish children. Thankfully, some years later, Side by Side opened, providing excellent facilities for able and less able children to learn and play together.

Ravenswood Village in Berkshire, of course, has its own school (for children who live in the village) and they are pioneers of special education in the Jewish community.

Pitching the religious atmosphere of Kisharon so that all the children and their parents would feel comfortable was a huge challenge for us. Judaism can be likened to a ladder on which one can find people on every rung of religious involvement. Thus the question arose – where should Kisharon pitch its level?

A high percentage of children came from traditionally religious homes and we decided that the school would mirror the home atmosphere that was familiar to the majority of them. As it happened, all the children loved and thrived on the resultant warm atmosphere. They were enthralled with preparations for Shabbat and festivals which permeated the entire curriculum.

The buzz expression at the time was 'cross curricular education' and that is exactly what we were able to create and maintain. The Jewish festivals round the year were reflected in nearly all the subjects. We made *matzot*[1] for *Pesach*, describing first how wheat grows, and cheesecake for *Shavuot* (the story of milk production). So with very little effort the children gained a fairly wide general knowledge of the world around them.

Later, wherever we could, we followed the national curriculum but for most of our children activities of daily living: dressing, washing, social skills, formed a vital part of their learning programme and, of course, binding everything together – Jewish social skills.

We wanted our children to be able to join in at the *Shabbat* and *Yom Tov* table and to participate in *shul*, as well as to get on with anyone they met in the world at large.

We had one little boy, Ari, who came from a fine family. The parents were not so observant, but Ari loved our programme so much that his parents began to take a real and active interest in a more observant way of life. For Ari's Bar Mitzvah, his parents hired a marquee, ordered a kosher catered lunch and arranged with us to stay with Rabbi and Mrs Plancey who had taken a great interest in Ari and Kisharon. The hospitality at the Plancey home was very special and added greatly to our day.

After lunch, to my amazement, Ari's mother did a perfect

---

1. During Pesach – the 8-day Passover festival – *matzot* are eaten instead of bread. During the Shavuot Festival that follows Pesach after seven weeks, it is customary to eat dairy food.

imitation of me leading *Birkat HaMazon*[2] the blessing made after the meal. The whole family, led by Ari, sang it from start to finish exactly as we sang it at school. It was really hilarious and so heartwarming. When the children returned to school after each festival, Ari would wriggle in his seat expectantly and ask, 'Now, what's next'?

The parents often told me how much they appreciated our efforts to teach the children as much about our Jewish way of life as possible. Each Friday they took home pictures and questions on *Parashat HaShavua*, the weekly bible portion, that the parents could discuss with them at the Shabbat table. This was the big plus of having children with special needs going to a Jewish school: they were the same as their brothers and sisters in as many ways as possible. They engaged in similar school activities and our children were familiar with their siblings' vocabulary, even if they could not express themselves as well.

This then was our ethos and it kept us very busy, happily so as we saw our pupils lap it all up and grow in confidence, feeling at home wherever they went.

Getting Out And About

Our school week was crammed full of activities. We had two minibuses whose drivers were exceedingly popular with the children. Malcolm, Bob and Len, to name just a few, had a wonderful way with the children, very much on a par with the teaching staff.

All the older children attended a mainstream school once a week and joined in either Physical Education or art lessons. They really enjoyed these visits, although sad to relate very few mainstream pupils made an effort to befriend our children

---

2. Birkat Hamazon is the Grace after the meals.

out of school.

The exception was David Sharman, who often took some of the boys for a walk on Shabbat and joined us for *Oneg* – the weekly pre-Shabbat activity – whenever he was in town. Even after he'd grown up and left home to study, he would ring me at home every festival to ask after everyone, and this continued until he married. Pupils also came every Friday from the Menorah Primary School in Golders Green to enliven our Oneg with their singing and dancing.

Horse-riding was one of the most popular activities, but it was quite difficult to get enough places for our children. At the stables the children were expected to feed, groom and clean the horses and they managed very well. One boy with an unpredictable temper was banned. When I asked why, I was told, 'The horses are frightened of him'! It was a great learning experience for all the children as they learnt to care for and respect the animals and to follow instructions.

Each week we were joined by several dedicated volunteers for our dancing class. Each girl had a partner and, with the music therapist at the piano, we all had a wonderful time.

We opened and closed the session with the 'Blue Danube' waltz and then practised some ballet steps, led by Shoshana Marks who had us all dancing to well-known pieces of music. Till this day I feel nostalgic whenever I hear the 'Carnival of the Animals'. Rosie Nevis came too and, under their guidance, we learnt country-dancing, line-dancing and, of course, wedding dances. I joined in each week and our ever popular volunteers ensured that any girl who needed help received it.

Edith was a faithful regular and also Judy Price. Judy passed away recently and was deeply mourned by us all. She was there for so many of our school activities, helping out in

Activities and Curriculum

Unable to even sit up, but a few years later – up and painting!!

her quiet way and being a real friend to the children.

Once a year Judy held a luncheon at her home in aid of Kisharon, and Lionel, her patient husband, had to put up with our invasion of his home. This event proved so popular and well-attended that Judy moved it to Lauderdale Road Synagogue, where it was a pleasure to see the unique beauty of the *shul* itself with its exquisite hangings embroidered by the Rabbis wife.

As the children grew up, work experience was introduced and some of the local shops were quite cooperative and gave our students regular work for an hour or two each week.

All these activities helped our children use their social skills, become known in the community and gain in confidence. Above all, they learnt new skills which introduced some diversity into their daily routine.

Our 'Bet Aviezer Workshops', named after a student who perished in a fire, and most capably managed by Yaacov Cramer and Jeffrey Gilbert, also flourished and continued to do so after I left. The students made cards for all manner of occasions and also laminated *Birkat HaMazon* cards, very often for weddings. A small gift next to each place at a wedding bearing the label 'Packed by Kisharon' made us all feel so proud that our students could, given the chance, make a contribution.

Bet Aviezer Workshops also had a bicycle repairing section and became well-known for their work in the community.

Once a year, one of the local Synagogues, the Golders Green Beth HaMedrash (GGBH), many of whose members served on our committee, prepared a *Melaveh Malka*[3] for our

---

3. The Melaveh Malka is a festive meal on a Saturday night after the Sabbath day. It is as if to say – farewell Sabbath – see you next week!

older students. Mrs Marilyn Posen arranged a beautiful meal and then there was always a musician and lively dancing. It was a real community occasion and our students talked about it for days. Rabbi Feldman, the Rabbi of the GGBH to whom we took all our problems, was the official school Rabbi.

Those students who would be overwhelmed by a large gathering were invited to a real family *Melaveh Malka* at the home of Mr and Mrs Danny Grunfeld. Each year the children felt more and more at home, thanks to our wonderful hosts. It was heartwarming to see our most disabled students, most of whom had little speech, relax and clap to the music and enjoy every minute. It was equally moving to watch our hosts' little children join in quite comfortably with their guests. This was 'inclusion' at its best and we were lucky to have such fine hosts.

Some parents also prepared a *Melaveh Malka* in their homes and these were greatly enjoyed by us all.

We were grateful to several of the local schools for helping us in a variety of ways. A very popular venture was the Kisharon Mobile Tuck Shop. Once a week a few of our older students went to 'Moishe's', our very friendly local shop and bought a supply of goodies. They packed it in little bags and, accompanied by their teacher, went to the Kerem School where the late Mr Dover had always been exceptionally helpful, integrating one of our pupils into his top class. Once there, our students set up their tuck shop and, when the Kerem children came out to play, they promptly bought up all the goodies.

This was a wonderful exercise in maths but, of course, the prime aim was to give our students a chance to use their skills in a fun way. One of the greatest skills one can acquire is the ability to get along with other people. This, above all, was what enabled our children to go out and about in a caring community.

Music

A school reflects its Head and Kisharon reflected my love of music. Over the years we were fortunate to have some superb music therapists. Whether they were Jewish or not, they all included in their repertoire the songs the children heard at their Shabbat table, during Yom Tov and in family celebrations.

Helen Smuts was our first therapist and during my last year as head teacher I worked with both Helen and Ruthie Shine playing music or dancing with the children.

We bought many kinds of percussion instruments and adapted well-known tunes to fit simple words. Using the instruments helped the children to learn to take turns, listen to each other, be part of a group, follow instructions and, above all, have fun in a productive, positive way.

As for me, it gave me the opportunity to work with each child and to get to know them really well – much better than the endless reports, thank you letters and phone calls awaiting me in the office.

Sit Like A 'Mensh'

I was visiting a school one day when I heard a teacher say to little boy of six, 'Sit like a *mensh*'[4]. He looked bewildered, as well as he might, until the teacher explained how she wanted him to sit properly on the chair.

At Kisharon we planned a clear programme of discipline to be used by the entire staff that was uniform throughout the school. There were a few what I might call 'no-nos' – absolutely no hitting or light smacking, no shouting, no sending out of

---

4. Mensh is a Yiddish word which can be loosely translated as a – well – mensh! A good and respectable person.

Activities and Curriculum

the room, and certainly no shaming a child in front of the class. So how did we manage?

For some odd reason, the bell in each classroom acted as a deterrent to bad behaviour. 'If you can't work nicely, I'll have to ring the bell'. I don't know why it worked as I was the mildest of head teachers and all I did was take the child to my office and give him something to do.

We tried to avoid confrontation until behaviour became out of control. 'Distraction' was a great tool and we often used it to divert a child from throwing a tantrum.

The main method, however, was to praise everything positive and try to ignore poor behaviour. All the children knew this and would say 'Ig' if a child was being 'stroppy'.

It worked like this: We're all reciting the Grace after the meal and one boy is banging his tabletop up and down. 'Ig, ig', chant the children, turning their eyes away and continuing to recite the grace with great gusto. Of course, the table banger feels very silly after a while and stops!

We had a little girl whom we wanted to wean of a certain poor habit. Together with the children, we did all we could to ignore (ig!) her. She persisted for two weeks (we almost gave up) but eventually she stopped completely. Strangely, she continued at home where the family found it impossible to 'ig', which was quite understandable.

Generally speaking, we tried to speak to the children clearly and always in the positive. Hence, 'Don't use your hands' became 'Please use your knife and fork'; 'Don't sit cross-legged on your chair' became 'Please put your feet on the floor' – certainly not 'Sit like a mensh'.

Children with Down's Syndrome often sit cross-legged. This is very harmful for their hips and is also socially unacceptable, for example in a bus or train. For one little boy who found it very difficult to sit with his feet on the floor we made a little mat so that he could see where his feet should be.

It is very important that children are given size-appropriate chairs so that, when seated with their backs supported, their feet reach the floor comfortably.

All this did not lead to perfect behaviour all the time, far from it, but we worked together as a team and that helped us to cope with most problems.

When we lived in England we often had our Israeli grandchildren to stay and one of them persisted in sitting cross-legged on her chair. To my request that she put her feet down she replied, 'Why? What difference does it make'? I had the perfect reply: '*Lo osim kach b'Anglia*' (it's not done in England). Now that we live in Israel and see her (and others) sitting cross-legged, I have to bite my tongue to refrain from saying 'Sit like a mensh'!

The Rings

We were always dreaming up interesting ways to encourage the children to learn proper 'social skills' – a euphemism for good behaviour.

With this in mind, I asked Malcolm, our school-keeper, to make a six-inch square board for each child and to fix ten hooks to each board. He attached a loop of string so that the boards could be hung on the wall.

When Malcolm had completed all the boards and hung them up in the classrooms, I went round with a bag of curtain rings and ceremoniously placed five rings on each board. I explained to the children that they each had a board with their name on it and they would start the week with five rings.

During the week they could gain or lose rings according to the effort they made with their work, behaviour and good deeds.

'Each week at the end of Oneg', I told the children with enthusiasm, 'each one of you will show me your boards. I will count the rings you have and for each ring you have on your board, you will get a sweet to take home'.

For weeks this worked well and the children sat entranced as I counted out the sweets into waiting bags – until I noticed that one young man was coming regularly with a board full of rings.

'Wow', I said, 'You must have done wonderful work this week'!

Lenny (for it was he of earlier fame), looked at me and then his infectious grin broke out.

'I pinched some rings from the other boards and', he added in his irrepressible way, 'I know where you keep them'!

Friday Discussion Group

As the boys (many of whom came from ultra-orthodox homes) grew up, it was no longer suitable for me to sing and dance with them, so the 'Friday Discussion Group' before Oneg ended my week in fine style. The boys sat around my office and we discussed any ideas or problems they might have with the school programme. Whenever there was a school event such as our annual holiday – the *Shabbaton* – on the horizon, our meetings became planning sessions during which we discussed menus, guests and programmes.

I loved this discussion group and the topics brought up by the boys enriched the school atmosphere and, above all, encouraged the boys to express themselves, take initiative, discuss, argue, plan, listen and be part of a group. Gradually, even the least verbal of the boys felt confident enough to contribute to the debate.

But the one who learnt the most was I – Head Teacher in the making.

Oneg Shabbat

Everyone looked forward to *Oneg Shabbat*[5]. It was one of my few 'No-nos' to say to a child, 'If you don't behave, you're not going to Oneg'.

Once I nearly broke this rule myself – but we had a problem and no solution. One of our younger children absolutely hated a certain song we sang quite often – she would open her mouth wide and howl! Each time it happened she had to be taken out for the sake of the other children, and I was very unhappy about this. So before Oneg I said to her, 'I want you to sit near the door and if we sing the song you don't like, don't cry, just go out'. It worked – we sang the song and she didn't budge. We never discovered why she hated it so much – indeed, she had a lovely voice and sang the other songs with great gusto!

We all sat in a circle and our music therapist and I prepared the programme, which we chalked up on the board.

The aim of the *Oneg* was to give the children and staff a fun ending to the week, but also to teach all the familiar Shabbat songs they would hear at home and in *shul*. We also took the opportunity to teach the children how to dance in a

---

5. The Oneg Shabbat, or Oneg for short, is a standard part of the Friday activities in Jewish Kindergarten around the world, it is a celebration of the oncoming Sabbath. The children and staff, sing, dance and hear about the key points of the Parshat HaTorah – the weekly portion of the Bible.

circle in preparation for the many weddings they attended.

For the same reason, we had a midweek dancing session. Happily, one of our students got married and as I danced with her she hugged me and whispered, 'Thank you for teaching me to dance'.

Of course, many of the children could not say the words of the songs and we also had several non-Jewish teachers, so I encouraged anyone who preferred to do so to sing la-la-la instead of the words. This worked very well for many of the children and I usually la-la-ed myself to get everyone into the spirit.

At the end of *Oneg* we sang out to each child as he or she left, 'Shabbat Shalom[6] to Chaim, Shabbat Shalom to Danny, Shabbat Shalom to Yosef, Shabbat Shalom'. This gave the children a thrill and they learned to wait their turn; as our Mister Lev often said, 'Let's make every moment a learning moment' – and we certainly did try.

Friday morning we had an Oneg for the very little children. About six of us sat in a circle and sang shortened versions of the regular songs and I danced with each child in turn. It was during this 'little Oneg' that Chaim learnt to get up onto his legs and move to the music. Until he was about five years old he could neither sit nor stand, but he was highly musical and the familiar tunes gave him the courage to put to use all he had learnt in his physical therapy sessions.

Once Chaim really became stable on his legs there was no holding him back. Passing through the lunchroom he could not resist pushing over a pile of plates and watching the result with an ear-to-ear grin. We quickly learnt to put the plates

---

6. The traditional greeting on Shabbat – Shabbat Shalom – a peaceful Shabbat.

higher up until the meal was served.

The running of the lunchroom was my special project. Almost every day until a few years before I retired, at 12.15 on the dot I turned into a lunchroom lady. The children were seated at tables according to their size and a member of staff sat at each table. I usually sat near a child who needed extra care or help with his behaviour.

We had a high counter and a lunch lady (we had several very lovely ones over the years) who put the food in tureens, one for each table. Each member of staff made sure that the children were sitting comfortably, feet on the floor and chair well up to the table.

The teachers probably thought I was mad as I went round pushing chairs close to the table, but the children could eat more cleanly that way and the food, in none too steady hands, went into their mouths and not on the floor. We encouraged the children to pass food around and chat to each other.

Chaim, of the broken plates fame, was a very late speaker and at first only spoke in a whisper. I usually sat beside him as he could only use one hand really well. One day he looked at their dessert and whispered to me, 'I want apple sauce'. I was so amazed that I asked the lunchroom lady to bring him some. After that, every time he did not like dessert, he repeated the performance. I blush as I write that whenever I sat next to him he got apple sauce. Strange to relate, no other child asked for this favour, probably because all the desserts were popular. We cooked the dairy lunch in school and tried to make it tasty, nutritious and kiddy-friendly.

The aim behind my organisation of the lunchroom was to prepare our children for eating with their families at the Shabbat and Yom Tov table. They learnt to wash their hands, say the *brachot*[7] and knew the whole benching by heart. Parents were delighted with all this and often told us that their child with special needs had better table manners than their other children. This structured lunchtime also made it possible to take the children to a restaurant or a wedding or just to a friend's house for a meal.

Lunchtime lasted 45 minutes, during which time the staff who were not on duty ate their lunch. When they finished they came to the lunchroom and took the children out to play for 45 minutes so that the staff who had served lunch could eat their meal. It worked well. When it was raining or very cold, the children watched videos in the library or looked at books.

I tried very hard to lead from the front, and was therefore with the children at lunch most days. That and teaching music to almost every class, helped me to understand the problems facing the staff and so we could work together as a team. As the poster in my office said: TEAM – Together Everyone Achieves *More*.

Shabbaton

Once a year we spent an entire Shabbat in school. 'The Shabbaton' was one of the highlights of the year. All the children joined in with the preparations and for weeks before made nash[8], challot and decorations. My Friday meetings with

---

7. Before eating bread Jews wash their hands and make a blessing (Bracha). After the meal they *bench* – say the grace after the meal.

8. Nash – goodies, Challot – special loaves of bread. Each Shabbat and on the festivals, at the start of every meal, a blessing is made on the Challa. It is cut on a Challa board using a Challa knife which are dedicated for this purpose. This is yet another

the older boys were devoted to the event and we planned weeks in advance whom to invite, who would sleep where and, above all, what to eat! It was an natural and effective way to encourage speech, thought, participation, speaking in front of others, listening within a group and, most importantly, initiative and enthusiasm.

The children brought their own sheets and blankets but we provided camp beds and air beds – the latter not a very good buy as, within five minutes, the children discovered how to deflate them. However, they had great fun on Friday taking them to the garage opposite and carrying them back fully blown up. We often had a good laugh at Kisharon. One of the best was when we moved into our new building at 1011 Finchley Road and noticed a large sign over the door of the garage opposite: 'Tyres and Exhausts'. 'Oh yes', said one of the teachers, 'We know that feeling'!

Friday night we had our own wonderful *davening* to which we invited the neighbours. We brought a huge stretch of curtain and, with hooks set in opposite walls and some strong wire, we could put up a very respectable *mechitzah* in a matter of minutes[9]. We also took this *mechitzah* on holiday with us (See section on Skeet). One year as we were preparing the Shabbaton at the school, we couldn't find the *mechitzah*. We hunted high and low, but to no avail. On Friday morning I sent someone to buy curtain net and a makeshift *mechitzah*

---

example of how religious life permeates every aspect of our Jewish life – and why it was so important for the children to be steeped in this tradition like their siblings.

9. In Orthodox communities, a mechitzah, a curtain, is set up between the men and women during the prayers. This segregated setting helps the congregants to concentrate in their prayers!

was up and ready just as we lit the Shabbat candles. Some months later, when we unpacked the Skeet equipment – there was the *mechitzah*. I had plenty to say to the person who had packed it by mistake!

We arranged the tables in a square shape and made them as beautiful as possible, taking special pleasure in arranging pretty flowers in tall wine glasses. After the first Shabbaton and many spilt vases, we filled the wine glasses with sand and water to keep them stable and fresh and presented them after Shabbat to the tired but happy members of staff.

Over the years we acquired lovely things to make our Shabbaton special: white tablecloths, challah covers, boards and knives[10] and *zmirot* (song) books. Those children who were able to do so prepared *Divrei Torah*, poems and readings. Others were delegated to lead the singing. We all took turns serving and clearing the meals and most of the staff stayed and enjoyed it as much as the children, which added to the *ruach* (festive spirit) and gave the children the opportunity to spend a delightful Shabbat in a happy, well-organised atmosphere.

After dinner we sat in a circle and guests came and sang with us or prepared a game. Who could forget Uncle Lenny (Leonard Finn) and his 'Itchy kvitchy meh meh meh'[11] or 'Mit my Musikalah'? Now, five years after retirement, whenever we get together for Shabbat, our grandchildren, without being reminded, only have to sing 'Mit my Musikalah' to give me a nostalgic thrill.

---

10. The challot are rolls made especially for the Sabbath. They are covered with a special cloth cover before the meal, and when eaten at the start of the meal, are cut using a special knife and bread board dedicated for this purpose.

11. Untranslatable!

Shabbat morning we were the guests of the Golders Green Beth HaMedrash and several of our boys were 'called up'[12]. Afterwards the ladies prepared a delicious *kiddush*[13] enjoyed by all.

Lunch was a lively meal, followed by a short rest (in theory) and games. Then came one of the highlights of our Shabbaton – we all trooped off to the home of Trevor and Inge Fenner for *seudah shlishit*[14]. Inge used to teach in the school and the children were thrilled to see her. She always prepared a delicious spread and, as this special day drew to an end and we sat round the table, I encouraged each of the children to make a speech of thanks to the Fenners and to express what the Shabbaton meant to them.

'Nice food, nice ice cream, thank you, next year – yes'?!

For me, this was a most moving moment. So many of the children had poor or little speech and yet they managed to thank everyone involved and to tell us just how much they appreciated the whole day.

After the speeches, with Inge surreptitiously digging into her box of tissues, we sang a lively 'Mit my Musikalah' and then *benched*[15] enthusiastically.

Trevor made *havdalah*[16] and then the minibus arrived to take us back to school. The day was truly unforgettable and remained a topic of conversation amongst us all for weeks. For

---

12. The GGBH was a local synagogue. On the Sabbath men are 'called up' during the reading of the Torah to make a blessing.

13. Refreshments after the prayers.

14. The last meal of the Sabbath, usually accompanied by the singing of traditional songs.

15. The blessing after the meal.

16. A ceremony that ends the Sabbath.

children whose social life was unfortunately very limited, this was the ultimate spin-off of our Shabbaton and a much-needed break for parents and siblings.

Bar Mitzvah And Sheva Brachot Celebrations

It is difficult to describe the closeness we all felt, staff to children, children to staff and staff to one another. Hence, when someone got engaged, a wave of excitement ran through the school. The thrill was only minimally less if one of the younger members of staff passed her driving test.

Often I was told in confidence that a teacher was 'going out' or had a driving test. I used to advise them, 'Don't tell anyone until the news is good'! A failed driving test meant a very sad teacher indeed and I always encouraged them to take them during the holidays!

However, when an engagement was announced, we straightaway began planning a sheva brachot[17]. Over the years we must have made dozens. Cecily and I would go out for tea and plan the menu. After that, I would leave it safely in her capable hands while I got on with my share in the event – the flowers, seating plan, decorations and music. These were memorable occasions with the full participation of the families involved. We never failed to be moved by the enthusiasm and happiness of our children.

---

17. During the week after a wedding, every day the Bride and Groom are invited to a 'Sheva Brachot' – a festive meal in honour of the newlyweds.

Kisharon

One fine day four Girls and boys went to Kisharon for a very special sabbath assembly we were greeted warmly and were shown around the school. The atmosphere was lovely. We talked to the teachers and the children. Everyone was so happy and frendly During their assembly they sang and danced. The mood was so festive. It was soon time to (go) say Bye we went back to our Menorah taking with us memories of a happy day. Thankyou Mrs Lehman. for a lovely afternoon. with best wishes

Nosson Planley

Notes from the students.

Naftali Goldberg   Kisharon   Hasmonean Prep.

When I arrived at Kisharon, I felt a very homely atmosphere. After staying there, and listening and seeing the children I felt I was crying inside. Tears began to swell up in my eyes, as I saw how much affection and love they needed and how much the helpers cared for them. They gave each child, an equal amount of their love. I felt very privileged to see these children and have such a fantastic experience. I tried to hide my tears, as I danced and sang, and tried to think of how much happiness, we were giving the children. Just before we went, the teachers sang a song to everybody's name, and that really, made me feel how much we were all together, and that the children we had seen were our brothers and sisters.

Part Three
The Kisharon Heroes

Parents Are Our Partners

In the 26 years I was involved with Kisharon, we were fortunate in working with very cooperative and caring parents. 'Parents are our partners' became our motto. Once a year the relevant staff together with the parents had a full review of each child and went over all aspects of the child's welfare, accomplishments and future needs.

We began by going over the 'resolutions' we had made the previous year, discussing what had been achieved and what was still outstanding. We then followed a written agenda to cover all areas of progress: scholastic, health, behaviour, family issues and transport. The next step was the formation of a new set of 'resolutions' around which the child's programme would be built.

During the year, of course, we spoke to the parents often and the teacher reported in the child's daily home-book anything interesting or special that had happened. Similarly the parent could write in the home-book if the child had had a bad night or anything else we needed to know.

Some parents made very good use of the home-book, while others were happy to leave the job to us, but generally speaking it was a very good tool for fostering school-home relationships. Occasionally, a child went through a very bad patch; in those cases we spoke on the phone in the evening and even made house calls if necessary. One crafty young man threw his book out of the window of the coach when he knew he was 'in trouble'.

Five years after my retirement I am still in touch with some of these wonderful parents. Our students are now adults and their parents are facing new problems. It is painful for both parents and their underachieving child to watch the other children leave home to study, marry and set up their own families. No such agenda is possible for the child – now adult – who is different. And grandchildren, though a delight, can cause stress and jealousy to their less fortunate aunts and uncles.

Parents themselves are now bravely and dynamically tackling this problem and many new schemes such as *Tikva*[1] are emerging. The parents who set up Tikva are those very same parents who brought their children to us in 1976. (I referred to them earlier in the book as 'the real pioneers'.) Once again they were unafraid to move forward with a new idea, this time their own. Tikva offers evening, weekend and holiday activities for their sons and daughters, while arranging supportive groups for the parents.

A few years ago, Chief Rabbi Jonathan Sacks kindly asked me to take part in his annual Rosh Hashanah BBC broadcast. I agreed, provided that members of Tikva would have the opportunity to speak about their work.

In completely unrehearsed filming in the home of one of our students, we outlined the work of Tikva and one of our

---

1. The Hebrew word for 'hope'.

students was delighted to sing and play with the Chief Rabbi, who put us all at our ease. It was highly gratifying to be included in the Chief Rabbi's inspiring programme, which told about people who had made a difference to life around them. *Tikva* members were specially encouraged by it and hopefully will now go on to think about residential provision.

Sheltered housing is the answer for some young adults and, run properly to a high standard, could relieve the parents of many of their worries, not least of which is, 'What happens when we are no longer here to care for our child'?

1011 Finchley Road

In 1984, I discovered that a large building up the road was for sale. We had really outgrown our present rooms, so this was indeed exciting news.

Our chairman, Mr Bentley, often came to school and asked to know everything about the children. In this way (and others) Mr Bentley was unique. I carefully broached the subject of our need for more space and told him about the building that had come on the market further up the road. He was immediately interested and promised to look into the matter.

Some time later, following months of discussions, friendly arguments and intensive planning sessions, we took possession of 1011 Finchley Road in Golders Green. The large corner building needed modernising throughout and, with the help of our architect Michael Katz and wonderful builders, the work proceeded with a great deal of enthusiasm all round. Michael would knock on my door in the evening holding a selection of tiles. 'Quick, choose a colour. They're starting the bathroom tomorrow'!

The Laughter And The Tears

Lady J (Amelie Jakobovits) at the opening of 1011 Finchley Road. Israel Ambassador Yehuda Avner is next to her.

Just before we were ready to move in with the children, we had a brilliant idea. A rather severely disabled boy would soon be bar mitzvah[2] and his parents were at a total loss as to how to deal with it or, in fact, to do anything at all. Yechiel could not read or write, could use only one hand and had little and very unclear speech. What he did have was a sparkling smile and a friendly manner which endeared him to everyone.

'Let's have Yechiel's bar mitzvah in the new building', I suggested to the staff.

'Good idea', they all agreed, resulting in a phone call to the long-suffering Michael.

'Michael, we have Yechiel's bar mitzvah in a few weeks. Will we be able to hold it in the new building'?

Silence on the line, and then, 'Well, if all goes to plan, I don't see why not'.

Everything *did* go to plan, thanks to Michael, who put his whole heart into the project from the first day. We prepared the hall and kitchen for our very first bar mitzvah and it became the pattern for all the bar and bat mitzvah events that were to follow, although each one was different and special.

Yechiel's bar mitzvah took place on Thursday morning.

---

2. A bar mitzvah is a celebration of starting manhood when a boy becomes 13. A similar ceremony – the bat mitzvah is made for girls when they reach the age of 12. This is not simply a birthday party. A mitzva is the Hebrew word for 'commandment'. When a boy reaches his bar mitzvah and a girl reaches her bat mitzvah they are considered adults and must keep all the commandments. The bar, or bat mitzvah is a major milestone and highlight in the development of a Jewish child who is now at the start of adult life.

Kisharon's new building.

We turned the lunchroom into a *Beth Medrash*[3] and the hall was perfect for the *seudah*[4]. Yechiel had practised his brachot and said them in tandem with his teacher. He was smiling so much that he could hardly get the words out – while we teachers, parents, family and fellow pupils looked on with happy pride. The occasion touched every heart and brought our new building to life.

After *shacharit*[5] and a *lechayim*, we took our places in

---

3. The word actually refers to a 'place of study' – but it seconds as a small synagogue when necessary.

4. The celebration meal.

5. Shacharit is the morning prayer service. After the prayers all the participants raise a toast – a 'lechayim' in honour of the

the newly renovated hall, made all the more beautiful by the imaginative table decorations and signs specially prepared for the occasion by fellow pupils. We made a careful seating plan so that Yechiel was surrounded by family and classmates, the unpredictable and frisky pupils sitting between two teachers.

With Helen or Ruthie, our wonderful multi-talented music therapists, at the piano, Yechiel was 'played in', went slowly to his seat and, amidst an expectant hush and with a huge grin, made a *bracha* and cut the *challah*[6], which the older girls had baked.

Yechiel and his parents had planned a menu with us, and the teachers had prepared a lively programme of songs and poems about him. Mr Bentley greeted the guests and thanked all concerned.

The highlight during a day of highlights was undoubtedly when Yechiel presented his mother with a bouquet of flowers and managed to say a few words. He smiled and smiled while we, his teachers, family and friends, cheered and cheered and held back our tears.

I personally heaved a sigh of relief – we'd made it! Our first bar mitzvah was in full swing – it *was* possible, even for a boy with limited speech and abilities.

Soon after Yechiel's bar mitzvah we moved into our new building. It was on two floors and had a playground and hall. This added a whole new dimension to our programme. Throughout the school – including in my office and the entrance hall –

---

occasion and of the new adult.

6. At the start of the Shabbat meals and on other joyous occasion like a bar mitzvah, a 'challah', a ceremonial loaf of bread, is cut after a suitable blessing is made.

there were soft, low armchairs covered in colourful fabrics, and everywhere there were large pin boards.

Every possible care had been taken to squeeze in plenty of toilets and a fully-equipped bathroom. In our first building, a child in need of a good wash had to stand in an old butler sink and hold onto a bar on the wall. A real bath was a welcome luxury as some pupils were doubly incontinent. Over the years several children had found it difficult to get ready in the morning in time for the coach. So we told the parents to put a coat over their pyjamas and we would see to the rest. When they arrived, 'the rest' included a bath and breakfast!

This was just one of the ways in which we tried to help the parents as well as the child. In the '70s and '80s having a 'handicapped' child was difficult; it was not spoken about and for some parents just to see their child board the Kisharon coach was heartbreaking.

Children with special needs can have very challenging behaviour – kicking, screaming and biting in total frustration. One day one of the parents rang me and said, 'I don't know what to do. I can't face her coming home today. My husband is an ill man and I'm at my wits' end'.

'Don't worry', I told her. 'We'll keep her until six o'clock, give her supper and one of us will bring her home'.

During the course of that day the concept of REAP was born and became a regular and much-appreciated part of our programme:

R – regular
E – evening
A – activities
P – programme

And *everyone* 'reaps' the benefit!

One of our dedicated teachers, Gerald Lebrett, was happy to mastermind the REAP programme and several willing members of staff agreed to work the extra hours. Gerald came to Kisharon as a young volunteer. He was a natural with the children and I urged him to study special education. For once someone took my advice: Gerald obtained his degrees, went to yeshiva[7], married and ended up headmaster of the school!

REAP was soon followed by Sunday *cheder*.[8] These two programmes gave parents some welcome breathing space and time for their other children.

Although I have spoken about helping parents, the children also benefited. Children with special needs often cannot read, play or occupy themselves in any way at all; as one parent put it, 'He just sits there and *clotses*'. Other children in the street keep well away, leaving our children often bored and lonely.

Medical Matters

We had many responsibilities in Kisharon and for me the most formidable was ensuring that children were given any medication they required during the day. We had a double check-list. The teacher who gave the medication put a tick next to the child's name and I, when I saw the tick, added my own.

This worked well and we only slipped up once. The sorry task of ringing the parents after school fell to me, but they totally understood.

Some children, however, suffered from seizures and

---

7. College of Jewish Studies.
8. Sunday school.

needed special help. In the early days we were lucky to have Dr Adler Senior next door to us. He and Mrs Adler were most reassuring and I well remember the first episode when a child had a seizure. We carried him next door and Dr Adler immediately did what was necessary. His nurse, Rose Brager Faber, gave my arm a comforting squeeze and that small thoughtful gesture was just what I needed. Dr and Mrs Adler always reminded us that they were there for us and many of our children were their patients.

We also had school doctors. Initially Dr Nachshon looked after us and often dropped in informally to chat over any problems we had. When he emigrated to Israel, Dr Ann Robinson (my niece) took over and was always available for advice. She examined all the children and gave very interesting lectures to the staff about their own health.

A little girl prone to epileptic seizures had to be given medication anally if she had an episode. So the parents very kindly came to my home to teach me what to do if ... I won't go into details but after that, once a week, I practised on a huge teddy.

Teddy and I sat on the school steps (the medication had an awful smell) and I went over the routine. I broke open the glass capsule, draw up the medication with a syringe and injected the fluid into poor Teddy's rump via a thin rubber tube. Fortunately Teddy was my only patient as Batya never had a seizure at school and when we went on holiday we took a nurse with us. Today this type of medication comes in a form which makes it much easier to administer.

We were fortunate to be given some high-quality PE apparatus which pulled out into a square of ladders. Tandy, our multi-talented PE and woodwork teacher, was very caring and careful with the children, so I had no qualms about allowing them to use the apparatus during lessons and under strict supervision.

One day I heard loud screams and a bell ringing. I could see from the panel in my office that the bell had been rung in the gym which was next to my room. With some trepidation, I ran towards the hubbub and found Miriam howling on the floor.

Tandy was trying to calm her and told me to call *Hatzoloh*, the emergency medical service which operates in Jewish communities. They arrived very quickly and whisked her off to hospital with a suspected broken ankle. Apparently she had jumped, without warning, from the top of the ladder, despite having been told to climb down. Poor Tandy! It was several weeks before he could bring himself to use the apparatus again.

Miriam spent the Sukkot Festival in hospital with her parents by her side. They were very understanding and our insurance covered all their expenses. It was the only time we had used our insurance broker so I asked him to be as generous as possible. It was the only real accident we ever had. When I visited Miriam in hospital she yelled from one end of the ward to the other, 'I won't jump again, Mrs Lehman'. I have only admiration for Miriam's parents who behaved commendably throughout. I hope they received adequate compensation.

We were very grateful to Hatzoloh who were with us within minutes whenever we had a problem, large or small, and this knowledge gave me much-needed peace of mind, for which I am eternally thankful. One day a teacher fainted and, of course, we sent for Hatzoloh. When they left she told me, 'I woke up, saw these bearded men looking at me and was sure

I had died and gone to Heaven'!

She wasn't far wrong – they were indeed angels!

Asperger's Syndrome

One day we received a phone call from the local police station. 'We believe a bomb has been planted in your building'.

'What shall we do'? I asked.

'Up to you, Madam', he replied cheerfully.

'Right', I said. 'We'll bring the children to the police station, because they can't stand in the street'.

Fortunately we had very regular fire drills, so I rang the alarm and, as the children and staff trooped past me, I told each member of staff to walk the children to the police station which was just down the road. After seeing them on their way, the school-keeper and I looked round the building but all the doors were secure and we saw no evidence of an intruder. We were checking all the corners and cupboards when the phone rang again.

'Police here. Sorry, Madam, we made a mistake. It's another school, not yours'. Before I could think of a suitable reply, he continued, 'And don't worry, all the children are happily munching kosher crisps and biscuits we bought for them'!

When I 'came to', I was pleased about the incident. It was very good practice for those children who found it difficult to cope with change and a welcome challenge for the staff to work in an unusual and fraught situation.

Coping with change was especially difficult for Avi, one of our older boys who suffered from Asperger's Syndrome, but was otherwise more able than many of the other children. Once a week the older boys went to the local grammar school for ball games and exercises. One week, as the boys were preparing to board the minibus, the school phoned to say that the teacher had not come and we should not send the boys.

Unfortunately, the boys were already outside on the pavement. I explained the situation and all but Avi trooped back into school. He folded his arms, stood tall and refused to move. All manner of persuasion failed and he stood there, looking straight ahead, not moving a muscle. I thought quickly and said, 'All right, Avi, will you come shopping with me to buy some chocolate as a treat for all the boys'? He agreed and we set off for the various shops near school where I bought several things I needed (and some I did not).

With Avi carrying the heavy bags, we returned to school. 'Thank you so much, Avi', I said innocently. 'Please put the bags on my desk'. He gave me a baleful look, slowly and carefully hung the bags on the gate, folded his arms and once again stood tall staring into space. And there he remained until the coach came to take him home at 4 o'clock!

Although this could be classed as an amusing incident in the life of the school, it highlights the difficulties of someone who even though having high ability in some ways, having Asperger's Syndrome, cannot accept sudden change. It could be dangerous and is certainly frustrating for the family. It also brings home the fact that children with high ability and their families can be just as stressed and distressed as those having to care for children with more severe disabilities.

It was after meeting Avi for the first time that I went home and wrote the poem, *Humpty Dumpty,* which appears at the front of this book. He had been hit by a teacher in a mainstream school and from that point, stopped speaking.

Speechmaking

I often spoke about Kisharon in mainstream schools and, when talking about the this particular problem, I would ask the pupils, 'How do you think these children feel'?

The words came tumbling out and the teacher would write them on the board: lonely, bored, sad, depressed, frustrated, angry. How right they were!

I loved speaking to school children and youth groups and encouraged them to compare their own lives and abilities with the lives of children who had little or no speech. To help them put themselves into the shoes of children less able than themselves I asked them to act out various scenes; for example, to imagine how they would behave at home after a bad day at school – lost gym shoes, forgotten homework, unappetising lunch and so on.

With one child acting the part of the mother, the other child spun her a tale of woe all about his awful day. 'Mother' was usually very sympathetic and offered a hug, tea and sympathy, although I remember one occasion when the 'mother' greeted her 'child's' litany of complaints with, 'You get up those stairs and wait till I tell your father'!

After the first act of this small drama, I chose two other children to act the same scene and explained that this time 'our' child had also had a bad day but, without speech, he could not tell his mother about it. 'What might such a child do'? I asked them before they began their enactment. Eagerly they took up the challenge and responded; 'Cry', 'shout', 'have a tantrum', 'stamp feet'. It was challenging for the children, but also a real eye opener that left them quite sad and with plenty to think about. Over the years I watched some very dramatic, realistic examples of all these manifestations of 'our' child's frustration.

Speaking in public about Kisharon became an important part of my work. At the beginning I was a bundle of nerves, but gradually I became more used to it and was able to speak from the heart, with ease and without notes and (hopefully) effectively.

On one occasion I was asked to speak to a group of elderly people. 'Keep it light', I was told. 'You don't want to upset anyone'. I kept it light, told them a few humorous stories about our children, the history of the school and sat down. Thereupon an elderly lady in the front row rose to her feet and, dramatically pointing a finger at me and in obvious distress, said, 'You don't know what you're talking about. My handicapped daughter is fifty years old and my life has been one long hell'!

Many years later, I was privileged to be invited by the Duke of Devonshire, a patron of the school and a charming and unassuming man, to speak to some of his friends at his exclusive club in the West End. I told the story of the elderly lady and, towards the end, became quite emotional. The Duke stood up, held his arms out to me and comforted me with 'Oh, my dear'.

The Duke was an active patron and one day he came to school for lunch. Of course, we made an especially attractive meal and, when we had finished, one of the children presented him with a large wooden clock that the children had made in our workshop. I knew for a fact that the Duke owned so many clocks in his Chatsworth home that he employed a man just to wind them up and care for them all. However, we couldn't think of anything to buy him and the clocks were what the children were making at the time.

He stood up, held the clock carefully, thought for a moment and then declared, 'To him who hath shall be given'.

A gentleman indeed!

Her Majesty's Inspector - Kathy Bull

Kisharon was registered with the department of education from day one. This meant that we had to fill in a very detailed form annually and be subject to regular inspections. Unlike the OFSTED of today, we were not told how to prepare for this inspection, we were only given a date when our HMI Kathy Bull would come and inspect the school.

I was not unduly worried, being guided by the principle of not expecting staff to put on a show for visitors. But I did expect the school to be neat and tidy at all times, with regularly changed, interesting wall displays and a comfortable ambiance for the staff and children. The entrance hall had two very large pin boards and one of them was my responsibility. On one occasion, feeling devoid of ideas, I printed out the name of each child in bold letters on cards and pinned them up at random. The children loved it and it was a very simple exercise in sight-reading for everyone.

Many children would never learn to read, but they could sight-read if they saw the words often enough. I prepared a similar display of various supermarket bags (an idea pinched from another school) and that also proved very popular.

Hence, we were only semi-apprehensive when the great day dawned. I arrived at school an hour earlier and was busy with a duster and a can of Pledge when there was a ring at the door. Thinking it was a colleague, I gaily opened the door waving the can of Pledge! On the doorstep stood an immaculately dressed, slim lady bearing a very business-like briefcase. 'Kathy Bull, HMI', she announced, fixing me with piercing blue eyes.

'Good morning', I stuttered, clutching the Pledge. 'Just having a final touch-up for our big day'.

The blue eyes indicated that she was not amused. 'If you could just show me where I could sit', she said. I ushered her into our small but very well-equipped library and she accepted my offer of a cup of tea.

I flew into the back office, boiled the kettle and, somewhat flustered, hurried back with the tea. There sat HMI Bull with a clipboard on her knee and a ruler and pen in her hand. Without looking up, she said, 'I'm putting a line under all the children over the age of 14 – they shouldn't be here as your licence is only up to 14 years of age. They'll have to leave'.

'But Miss Bull', I protested, 'Department for Education (DFE) knows these children are here. We send you the details annually and we always receive an acknowledgement. Why were we not informed'?

'I'm talking about your licence, not your annual return. This is a serious matter and the children must leave as soon as it can be arranged'.

There followed days and weeks of agonised pleading with DES, all to no avail.

Birth Of Senior Centre One: The Coach House

The executive committee met and decided, after an exceedingly heated discussion, that, albeit unwillingly, we would accept the ruling. The staff and I were devastated. We could think of nothing else. There was no other Jewish educational provision for young adults.

Back to square one, I thought. Our older children would

be completely lost in a non-Jewish school: they can't eat the lunches, can't be in the Xmas play, again the problem of early Fridays and festivals and, above all, no Jewish education.

By chance I attended a lecture about the subterranean water system in Jerusalem and after the lecture I was introduced to the speaker, archaeologist Dr Stephen Rosenberg, who was interested to hear about Kisharon and our present predicament.

He was very thoughtful for a moment and then said, 'You know, it's strange that we met today, because a house in North Finchley has just come on the market and, because it's so dilapidated, it's going quite cheaply. It's a converted stable called 'The Coach House'. Why not turn it into a centre for your older pupils'?

The Senior Centre.

All this happened in May. By September we had opened our first senior centre in the Coach House on Nether Street in North Finchley. It was a compact house on two levels, but set in small but delightful grounds with several tall, shady trees and surrounded by a magnificent laurel hedge. With Dr Rosenberg's help, we had it beautifully renovated and our older students settled in very quickly. The name 'Coach House' stuck.

We had the official opening in November in the presence of the Mayor and HMI Kathy Bull. We had to put up a marquee for all the guests as the weather was freezing! As I reached the podium to make my speech, I quipped, 'I do hope, Mr Mayor, that, when we apply for planning permission to extend the building to include a hall, the members of the borough of Barnet planning committee will remember how cold it was in the marquee'! There was a roar of laughter – and even a smile from Kathy Bull.

As I showed Miss Bull around, I said, 'We should call this the 'Kathy Bull Centre'. If it weren't for you ...', her blue eyes glinted mischievously as she turned to admire the well-equipped kitchen.

Over the years I got to know Kathy Bull well and she was always very helpful, as long as we kept to the rules. In time our licence was extended so the children could stay in school till the age of 19.

Of course we had to find a highly-qualified manager for the centre and luckily, by word of mouth, I heard about Greig McNeish who was manager of a similar centre. We arranged to meet there.

With a wonderful Scottish accent and calm manner, he showed me around and his enthusiasm, as well as his professional qualifications and well-kept premises, got him the job.

Though not Jewish, Greig picked up our Jewish ethos very quickly. Together with his students, for example, they made the most beautiful murals about the weekly *sedrot*[9] and for the festivals. He introduced us to several effective teaching methods and soon had the students busily learning and enjoying age-appropriate activities.

Over the years we added a workshop in the grounds where the students made small wooden items, and a greenhouse where they learnt how to grow plants from seeds and cuttings. However, Greig's biggest hit was the rabbits.

I used to visit the centre every week to review the progress of each student and consequently was soon introduced to the bunnies. 'Don't worry, we won't be overrun', said Greig, 'They're sisters'. Someone got it wrong because before long we had about twenty bunnies hopping around!

Greig was a wonderful colleague and an excellent teacher. When he left to take up a senior position at the Autistic Society, we made him a farewell party and during my speech I mentioned just how well he had picked up our religious ethos. As I paused before my next sentence Greig piped up '*Baruch HaShem*'![10] – proving that he had picked up our language too!

As more students transferred to the Coach House, we had to think about a second building. I was not in favour of placing students who needed a great deal of personal care with those of high ability. Their needs were quite different. Each group

---

9. The weekly portion of the Bible read in the Synagogue on Shabbat morning.

10. Thank God.

needed an appropriate programme.

Again by chance (if anything is ever by chance) we heard that a synagogue in Edgware was closing down their nursery and wanted to rent their building. We went to see it and decided that, after adaptation, it would be suitable for our more able students. A few months later our second senior centre was opened in Edgware under the capable leadership of Rabbi Simcha Richland. We set up two workshops there, one for woodwork and the other for printing, bookbinding and allied skills.

Now I had two places to visit each week and they were the highlight of my busy schedule. The school now had a deputy head, David Goodman, so I had time to oversee the two senior centres. The managers were excellent and self-sufficient, but were happy to review matters with me once a week, mainly checking the students' progress.

David Goodman had originally come to us as a sports and physical education teacher and was very gifted in his relationships with the children. I encouraged him to further his qualifications and, despite a hard day's work, he took degrees in special education and took over as executive director the year before I retired. He also organised the highly popular annual sports day.

The parents of the older children were delighted that they did not have to agonise over where to send their child when he or she reached the age of 14 – but they *did* agonise over what they would do when they were no longer able to look after their child at home.

The Hanna Schwalbe Home

Quite by chance (again!) I heard of another house

going for a good price due to its very neglected condition. The long-suffering, charming Mr Bentley and his committee were by now becoming accustomed to my sudden ideas, so when I announced at a meeting, 'Some of our parents are interested in a residential home', they took up the challenge with enthusiasm.

Once again, with Michael Katz in the lead, we purchased and refurbished the property and opened our residential home. It was named 'The Hanna Schwalbe Home' after the grandmother of one of our students and was generously donated by his family.

So once again we stood by the school motto: 'Parents must not agonise "what next?"'

The opening of the Hanna Schwalbe Home was a huge step forward for Kisharon and yet another venture into uncharted waters. There were eight rooms furnished as 'bed-sits', one for each resident, and accommodation for sleeping-in staff. The house had a large living area, a small den and a huge U-shaped kitchen. One side of the U was furnished as a dining room with square tables that could be moved into the living area for Shabbat – used separately or linked together. The middle part of the U was the main kitchen and the third side had a fridge, tables and chairs, microwave and a door to the living room. I planned this area as a place where the residents could help themselves to snacks and entertain members of their families.

An outdoor games room was added later so that the boys (for they were all boys) could relax, play ping-pong and so on. The Hanna Schwalbe Home filled up very slowly. Parents found it extremely difficult to send their sons into residential care. The few girls also needing care went to a similar centre 'Yad

Voezer' in North London, whose founder, Mrs Landau, was one of my earliest inspirational advisors. Mrs Landau was the first person in the Jewish community to introduce light and sound therapy and patterning. Today, Yad Voezer maintains well-developed and excellently run residential homes, as well as a day care centre and other supportive services.

The Hanna Schwalbe Home's first manager was Amanda Moss, who had the challenging task of setting up a new venture for Kisharon and running it to a standard which would satisfy the various inspections. Today it is managed by Judy Meshulam and her hard-working team, who continue to maintain a high standard, passing council checks – announced and unannounced – with flying colours.

With the gradual occupation of the eight rooms, the boys learnt how to go shopping and produce nourishing meals and studied all the skills needed for the activities of daily living. Under Judy's guidance, the excellent staff turned it into a comfortable, warm home for the boys, in which they could grow and use all their abilities to the full. Judy led from the front. She loved the students and their welfare was her main concern. She looked after them with singular devotion and a great sense of humour which spread to the entire staff.

At about this time, parents asked us to open an integrated nursery and, although I thrive on challenge, I told David Goodman: 'You oversee the Hanna Schwalbe Home and I'll concentrate on establishing an integrated nursery'. In the early days of Kisharon we did have a small integrated group of able and less able toddlers, set up by Jackie Brewer. It worked well but, as the able children left to go into mainstream education, those less able formed a group by themselves and we had no further applications from able children.

The problem of integrating able and less able children is too vast to discuss in this book; suffice to say that, when the children are all toddlers, they can play and learn together quite well, given a high staff-children ratio. However, as pencil skills are introduced, some of the less able children fall behind and the gap widens.

Our second attempt, led by Kathy Bowker, a splendid person and teacher, began slowly but, once again, as soon as the toddlers reached school-age, the more able ones left to go into mainstream education.

After I retired, a group of parents opened an integrated nursery called Tufkid at a separate site and this thrived, probably because it was led by very determined parents who were role models for the rest of the community.

Skeet House

During one of my fundraising talks, I mentioned that our children rarely went away on holiday and neither did their parents. The often unpredictable behaviour and medical issues of children with special needs make holidays a very difficult undertaking rather than a pleasure.

After the meeting, a lady approached me and said that her uncle, Yoggi Mayer, was very involved in Skeet House, a large country manor near Orpington, Kent, which had been specially adapted to provide holiday accommodation for children. The next day I rang Yoggi, who was delighted to hear about Kisharon and offered to take me to see the property the very next day.

Skeet House is a very old building set in acres of lawns and shady trees. It includes a tennis court, a football pitch and an indoor swimming pool. Yoggi's enthusiasm was infectious.

I returned to school and discussed with the whole staff the possibility of a holiday in Skeet. I must have caught Yoggi's enthusiasm, because we all agreed to make a booking first and to discuss details later. The parents were delighted to hear about the proposed holiday and agreed to allow their children to come from Monday to Friday. Thus began some of the happiest times in the life of Kisharon for staff and pupils alike – and me!

Several teachers couldn't come, of course, as they had small children, but our Limudei Kodesh staff were all young girls and were thrilled at the idea. We realised that, in order to look after our children properly, we would need a one-to-one staff-student ratio, plus a cook. Over the years we had the most wonderful young boys and girls accompanying us as volunteers. They were the life and soul of the party and became fast friends with all of us. Most of them acquired real skill in caring for our children, and our children loved them all.

We had already taken small groups of children to Carmel College, so we had some idea of how to prepare for the holiday – but, oh, how much we learnt the first time 35 children and staff went to Skeet House!

The first year we left it to the parents to send whatever clothes they liked in whatever bags they wanted. When I saw those enormous suitcases arriving, I had to send for two strong boys to help us lug the cases up to the top floor.

The following year, much the wiser, we provided each child with a large chequered zipped bag which we had bought in the market. Each bag had a label with the child's name and the name of the room where he or she would be sleeping. Each room had a name of a village in the surrounding area. In the bag we put a clothing and equipment list with the

Enthusiastic phone call home from Skeet House holiday.

polite suggestion that no fancy clothes, no nash and only one beloved soft toy be included! We also asked that the bags be returned after the holiday, folded neatly into a flat square to ensure easy storage.

Over the 25 years that I went to Skeet, most parents cooperated, but we all became dab hands at folding those bags. They were so strong and light that before long we bought more and packed all our cooking gear, games and everything we needed into what became known as 'Skeet bags'.

A small group of us went down on the Sunday before the holiday began to make the beds and generally prepare the house and cook the first meal. Skeet House had a caretaking couple who lived in a small house in the grounds. Over the years we had different couples who were, on the whole quite helpful. One year, when we arrived on Sunday, there was a new couple in the house. We introduced ourselves and then got busy preparing the kitchen. Suddenly we heard the most awful screams and, running up the stairs in the direction of the noise, we found the cleaning lady looking white and shocked.

'I saw the ghost, I saw the ghost', she cried.

'What's it like'? I asked curiously, as Yoggi had told me that Skeet House was reputed to be haunted by a ghost called Lady Cynthia.

'She's a little old lady with her hair up in a bun and she was wearing a riding habit', replied the cleaner in a shaky voice.

By then the caretaker had arrived on the scene. 'Is that right'? I asked. 'Is that what the ghost looks like'?

'I don't know', he said, 'but I'll ring Yoggi and ask him'.

He returned looking rather green. 'Well', we all asked in chorus. 'What did he say? What does the "ghost" look like'?

He looked at us for a few moments as he tried to get the words out. Finally he spoke. 'Yoggi says she's a little old lady with her hair up in a bun and she wears a riding habit'. Interestingly enough, we learnt later that this 'ghost' was well documented and is written about, in a book about Skeet House and also in documents housed in the local library.

However, we had a great deal of work to do, so we made cups of tea for everyone, especially the shattered cleaning lady and somewhat dazed we returned to our work, making the beds and preparing the kitchen and food for the first meal. It was hard work, but when all was finished we made ourselves a delicious snack and relaxed under the trees, enjoying the quiet country atmosphere. We all enjoyed preparing Skeet and I had no problem recruiting volunteers to join me.

The children, staff and volunteers arrived at teatime on Monday, having first been to some local attraction and having enjoyed a picnic lunch. Tea on the terrace – with big hugs for us and high spirits all around – signaled the beginning of our holiday.

Each day we had a fixed rota and timetable: Breakfast, *davening*,[11] outing with a picnic lunch, followed by swimming and relaxing activities until supper-time.

After supper there was *davening* and then we all gathered in the sitting-room and enjoyed an evening of singing and games. We were always lucky enough to have with us the current music therapist or a teacher who could play the guitar. Denah and Ruthie came year after year and greatly added to our evenings with the children.

Those evenings are precious in my memory. The children were so relaxed and happy and exhibited very few behaviour problems. They willingly took turns to sing solo, make a speech or generally add to the fun and warmth of the evening. The sitting-room had wood panelling and a very high old-fashioned fireplace. Armchairs were scattered all round the room while some of the younger children sat on the cosy carpet in their pyjamas. The atmosphere was such that even today, many years later, whenever I meet colleagues from that period, we are soon swapping memories of Skeet and the children who meant so much to us.

Each child was twinned with a member of staff or a volunteer for the whole holiday so, after a final singsong ending with 'HaMalach HaGoel', the children were escorted up to bed and settled down (hopefully) for the night. One by one, the staff returned to the comfortable armchairs, made coffee, brought out some nash and relived the wonderful day. We invariably ended the evening with an evaluation of the day

---

11. Prayers.

and plans for the next one.

We always took a cook with us and planned tasty dairy meals. One of the day's 'chores' was making the sandwiches for each day's outing. I often masterminded this and any fellow sandwich-maker reading this will remember how I fussed around, making sure that the slices was taken out of the packet in twos and then opened like a book so that, when the filling was put in, the sandwich closed neatly. Quite a few of the children had poor grip so the sandwich had to be easy for them to handle.

The fillings were chosen by the older boys during our pre-holiday Friday 'meetings'. The sandwiches were wrapped in foil, labelled and included special instructions, such a 'no filling for Chayim', or some such strange request. It was the children's holiday and we spared no effort to keep them happy and content.

One year the cook let us down at the last minute. Our son Rafi, who was self-employed at the time, offered to cook for us on one condition: 'That you don't come into the kitchen'! he informed me. At that stage, I would have agreed to almost anything, but made one condition of my own: that the job would include shopping for all the food, preparing the kitchen, serving and clearing up! I can't remember what Rafi replied, but I do remember that we had mouth-watering, precision-served meals, with the added bonus of discovering that Rafi was a natural with our children. The children loved him and he came for quite a few years, helping out in many different ways. Today he is a volunteer at Alyn.

Several years later, long after Rafi was married and had his own children, we were at a wedding together and happened to meet some of our Kisharon children, now grown up. Ignoring

The Laughter And The Tears

me completely, they made a bee-line for Rafi, shouting, 'Rafi, Rafi, do you remember Skeet'? It was one of many emotional moments of my life with Kisharon.

Although I was not in charge of any particular child, I went on all the outings. My role was to keep an eye on the kitchen, make sure that the programme never flagged and cope with any problem involving a child or member of staff.

Each year the programme was different, but often included Lego Land and Thorpe Park. As I got older (I went over twenty times to Skeet), my folding chair became an essential part of our luggage. I would find a nice spot to sit, surrounded by the sandwiches, drinks and medical and first-aid equipment, while everyone else went off to enjoy the rides and attractions.

This was an important breather for me and also an opportunity to write the daily diary, a copy of which went home with every child. This was greatly appreciated as many of the children had little or limited speech and it was vital that the parents could talk to them about their week at Skeet.

Naturally, most days someone stayed with me, perhaps a child not feeling so well or just refusing to go. Ronny was one of those who insisted on staying with me on one occasion. Next to us was a huge bouncy castle. Happily jumping up and down were thirty little girls, all in uniform: cute pleated skirts and white panama hats. Sitting with me was Malcolm, our caretaker/handyman and a great friend of the children. I asked Malcolm to show me something on my new mobile phone and in a split second Ronny was up and away and heading towards the plug of the bouncy castle. Out came the plug, down came the castle and thirty squealing little girls went sprawling, panama hats flying in all directions!

I don't recall the details of my apology – but I do

remember a contrite Ronny sitting next to me cross-legged, wringing his hands as only he could, and murmuring, 'Poor Mrs Lehman, poor Mrs Lehman'! I remained quite calm; after all, I should have known. Ronny had a wicked sense of humour and a store of pranks, 'Poor Mrs Lehman' being his oft-heard mantra. When he was very young he loved to flush his *kippah*[12] down the toilet, watching with glee as it swirled around out of sight. 'Whee', he would chortle, 'Whee – all gone. Poor Mrs Lehman'.

His favourite trick, however, was to open the cupboard under the sink, unscrew the U-bend and turn on the taps. Above the gushing water we could hear him chanting, 'Poor Mrs Lehman, poor Mrs Lehman'. It remains a mystery how he managed his pranks in a well-staffed classroom. Today Ronny is a grown man, loved by all, but still up to his tricks. Lucky Mrs Lehman to have known him!

Last Day At Skeet

The last night at Skeet was very special. We served a delicious salmon meal with all the trimmings. All the male members of staff disappeared to prepare the annual play. No script, no rehearsal, no scenery, just a few simple props and costumes and we were ready to begin. Over the years we tried several stories, but Cinderella was the most popular. We had many volunteers at Skeet and during their pre-holiday interview they were always bewildered by the first question: 'Can you act'?

With a teacher perched on a high stool narrating the story, one of the music therapists at the piano and children and staff

---

12. Skull cap – a head covering worn by boys and men.

sitting in rows, the show was on. Over the years we had some wonderful Cinderellas, but it was the ugly sisters who stole the show. How we all laughed! The story always ended with a *chupah*[13] for Cinders and Prince Charming, with a great deal of audience participation from the children.

The next morning, following *davening* and breakfast, half the staff cleared up the house and packed our equipment, pots and pans, while the others played with the children on the lawn. When all was ready and the Skeet bags were lined up next to the waiting coaches, we sat in a circle on the lawn. One by one we asked the children to say a few words. They were masters at the art of speech-making – short and to the point:

'Thank you, teachers'.
'Thank you, Mrs Lehman'.
'Lovely food'.
'Lovely outings'.
'Come again soon – yes'?

They loved Skeet – and so did we! I will always remember the dedicated teachers and volunteers who worked so hard to give our children such a fun-packed holiday – but what made it really special was that we enjoyed it too and recall it with nostalgia whenever we meet.

Long after I retired and just a few days before we went on *aliyah*[14], two members of staff, Judy and Ruthie, rang up to say they wanted to take me out for a farewell supper of fish and chips (my favourite food!). 'Be ready at six', they said. 'We'll call for you'.

They arrived on time and off we drove – and drove and

---

13. Marriage canopy under which the bride and bridegroom stand during the wedding ceremony.
14. 'Going up' or emigrating to Israel.

drove and drove! Suddenly I began to recognise the scenery. We were in Kent! They were taking me to Skeet! Through the tunnel, past the tolls into Orpington and then up the narrow winding Skeet Hill Lane to Skeet House.

It was quite dark by then and the house was shrouded by the tall trees we knew so well. Not a light showed as we got out of the car and they ushered me onto the patio where we had often served tea to the children. Before I could say a word, they opened a big bag and out came a tablecloth, flowers, candles, plates, knives and forks, a thermos flask of tea *and* fish and chips! Had it not been fish and chips, I would have been too overcome to eat. They told me that they'd asked the caretaker for permission to bring me, but he'd replied with an emphatic 'No', which made our moonlit meal all the more exciting as we wondered who would find us first, the caretaker or the 'ghost'!

I had been to Skeet probably 25 times, but this particular visit symbolised the unique friendship that exists among everyone who worked at Kisharon and loved our children.

Off To Israel – 1991

As the school, the two senior centres and the Hanna Schwalbe Home, led by their capable managers, all settled down and, encouraged by the success of the Skeet enterprise, I suddenly had a wonderful idea: Why not take a small group of older children to Israel for a holiday! This trip, which constituted a very special two weeks in my life, deserves a whole chapter to itself.

Once I have an idea, I cannot rest until things start moving – so off I went to receive the blessing of the committee, the agreement of the parents and, above all, staff participation.

We decided to take Lenny, Rivka and Benny, accompanied by Rina and myself. At the time my educational adviser Nora Gates, the retired head of a special education school and by now a good friend with a saucy sense of humour.

'If I pay all my expenses, can I come with you to Israel'? she asked. I was surprised and pleased. Nora was not Jewish but she had considerable experience in travelling with less able children and I was happy she could come.

So in 1991, with everyone cheering us off, we set out in the minibus for Heathrow. We said goodbye to Bob our driver and led three very excited students into the airport.

We thought we had prepared our children well, but apparently not well enough. 'Who packed your bags'? the security person asked Benny. 'None of your business', he snapped back! I hastily explained the situation in Hebrew to the El Al personnel, who were quite speechless for a moment or two though, one was sure, most amused and no doubt 'dined out' on the story for months.

After an uneventful journey, which the children managed very well indeed, Richard, who was to be our guide and security person, met us and led us to a beautiful, roomy seven-seater car. After introducing everyone to Richard, we took our seats while he stashed our luggage away.

Our first stop was Givat Washington, where my sister-in-law, Lily Robinson, was in charge of a group of English children from the JFS School in London who were in the middle of a three-month stay in Israel. This is an appropriate point to record that it was Lily who persuaded me to go back into teaching after a fifteen-year gap and, had I not taken her advice then in 1972, I would not be writing this story now.

We were given several comfortable rooms and soon

unpacked and settled in. Nora was an old hand at travelling with less able children and she soon had us organised and ready for our first trip the next day to the Tel-Aviv beach and then to a museum. Used to spending hours making sandwiches whilst at Skeet, it was a real treat to be able to go out knowing that we could eat in most places.[15]

Richard was an ideal guide; he sensed when the children became bored, piled us back into his car and took us to the next place. We planted trees, we visited several museums where the children identified with all the Jewish artifacts and we strolled through the streets of Jerusalem.

While looking at the Dead Sea Scrolls, Benny remarked with great excitement, 'It looks like the inside of a mezuzah or a *megillah*'.[16] I was so proud of him and it was a far more appropriate remark than the one he'd made at the airport!

At some point I said to Richard, 'I'm sorry if parts of your commentary are lost on some of our children'.

'Don't worry', he said, 'I've taken world Jewish leaders around Israel and your children know more than they do about

---

15. Keeping to a strictly Kosher diet means that it is difficult to 'eat out' – so any outing always involved taking food with us. In Israel many of the restaurants and fast food shops are Kosher, so eating out is not an issue.

16. A mezuzah, which contains a parchment with a verse from the Bible, is fastened on the right hand side of the entry of the house and each of the rooms, usually in a decorative covering. The megillah is a scroll with the story of the Persian King Achashveros and his evil adviser Haman who tried to destroy the Jews, They are outwitted by the Jewish Queen Esther and her uncle Mordechai. This story is read with great pomp once a year on the Purim holiday. On Purim, children dress up – often as Esther or Mordechai. It is one of the highlights of the year, especially for children.

the Jewish religion'. I was so pleased about his comment, and it was perfectly true. To our children, Judaism wasn't just in books – it was their way of life. I thought to myself that it was worth all the anxiety and effort we experienced making sure our students could stay in Kisharon once they were 14 years old enabling them to take advantage of this special trip to Israel.

The following week we drove into Jerusalem where we were due to stay at the Kings Hotel. We had warned Nora that wherever she went she must be prepared to present her handbag for security inspection. So, while we were escorting the children into the Kings Hotel, she meekly handed her handbag over to the 'security' man, who promptly ran off with it into the crowded street. Poor Nora. 'But Chava, you told me to show my bag', she said.

Nora was leaving us the next day and was now without money, passport or tickets. I can't remember how we all coped, but she did go to Switzerland the next day and told me gleefully on the phone, 'I can "dine out" on this for months'! Nora was a gifted teacher and a good sport. When I asked her how much first aid I should take on the trip, she took out of her bag a small purse containing a few plasters, cough sweets and baby aspirin. 'You'd be surprised at the magical recuperative powers of half a baby aspirin', she said smiling.

Lenny, Rivka and Benny were thrilled with their holiday. The highlight for them was buying gifts for their families. The highlight for me was the joy at knowing that, with minimal help, children whom society classed 'special needs', 'learning disabled' or whatever was churned up as the latest 'label' were perfectly able to function away from home. Now they had something to talk about, just like their siblings. They, too, for one glorious fortnight, had been part of the crowd, part of normal life – no longer looking in from the sidelines in silent loneliness.

Finance

All these activities – holidays, therapies and outings – cost a great deal of money of course and the question was often asked: where did the money come from?

From the moment we received the £5,000 seed money from the Chief Rabbi's Office, I tried to stop worrying. So many people helped us. Today, thrift shops are a feature of every high street, but in 1976 they were unheard of. My good friend Claire Caplan rented a large empty shop on Golders Green Road (I think it is now McDonalds), acquired clothes racks and tables and went around collecting clothing and bric-à-brac. With a money apron round her waist and some trusty helpers, within a fortnight she had raised a great deal of money.

Claire also helped in the school and the children loved her and called her 'Mrs Capstan'. She organised a dinner for us without all the expensive trimmings of later dinners and every penny raised went to Kisharon.

Dennis and Nadine Rosenthal arranged highly successful musical evenings, during which I showed slides of our fledgling school. Again refreshments were donated and every penny went to the school.

It became popular for school children to devise all sorts of novel ways to raise money for us. I imagine one of the more daunting fundraising ideas was the sponsored silence! They would come to the school and shyly present their little bundles of money. We would show them round and always made sure to write and thank them. I think our thank you letters were a form of secret weapon and they encouraged people to continue with their efforts on our behalf.

Perhaps the most innovative effort was the annual sale

of bones for the *Seder*[17] plate at Gross Butchers. When we received the generous sum raised (I suspect nicely rounded up by the late Brian Gross) I wrote a poem of thanks, which he displayed for his customers to see.

But above all, we were blessed with wonderful chairmen. Max Sulzbacher called the first meeting in his home against all odds and he was followed by Ken Gradon, Malcolm Wulwick and then the longest standing chairman of all Walter Bently. Our building chairmen, Jonathan Shleider and Bernard Goldblum were always kept busy as we bought yet another building, Fred Rosenberg and Bernard Trent looked after the finances and made sure that every member of staff was paid on time and that the children had the equipment they so vitally needed. Steven Greenman, the overall chairman, kept things running smoothly in his calm warm way while Yurie Curtis got everyone up and active with his wonderfully organised bike rides involving all the local schools.

One day I received a phone call from a social worker. She said she had an elderly client who was alone in the world. If I agreed to be her executor, she would leave her money to

---

17. The festival of Pesach (Passover) celebrates the emancipation of the Israelites from slavery in ancient Egypt some 3300 years ago. The 'seder' is a festive meal on the first night during which the parents relate to the children and to each other this momentous event. The 'seder plate' is a large plate at the centre of the table on which are placed several items that remind us of the slavery days and the freedom from that slavery led by the great leader Moses. The items include *charoset,* a sweet mix of apples, nuts and wine, *marror*, a bitter herb that reminds us of the bitter days – and a bone – that reminds us of the Lamb Sacrifice made on the eve of the exit.

The Kisharon Heroes

Kisharon. I agreed and thought no more about it until one Friday the social worker called again to inform me that Miss P had passed away and that I had to arrange the funeral for that day. I rang the relevant people and was told that the lady had not belonged to any burial society but, if I put £500 in the post at once, they would see to everything.

My husband was abroad at the time and I had no idea if I could write a cheque for that amount. Realising that I could not use school money, I rang the social worker for advice. '*Chas veshalom*[18] you should pay', she reassured me, 'Leave it to me'.

Poor, lonely Miss P was buried on a cold Friday morning. It was a very sad story and I was glad that she had been properly looked after in her last hours.

Weeks passed and I forgot the incident. One day an official-looking letter arrived. The work on Miss P's estate had now been completed and they were 'happy to enclose a cheque'. Sadly I looked at the cheque: £27. Poor, lonely Miss P, had she lived longer, she might have died of hunger!

We were constantly thinking up new ways to raise money and decided to order *pushkas*[19]. We chose bright yellow and were supplied with stickers and labels announcing: 'Kisharon Day School – please give generously'.

We spent hours attaching the labels and distributing them to various shops and families. Over the years we found some wonderful people who took upon themselves the job of emptying the boxes, affixing clean labels and writing receipts. This is a good opportunity to pay tribute to all our volunteers – too many to name individually.

---

18. God Forbid.
19. Charity boxes.

The Volunteers

Judith Lebrett was our volunteer organiser. If we needed extra help with swimming, horseback-riding or anything else, we rang her and she kept us supplied with dedicated, helpful volunteers. Judith also worked in the school and she and her husband Stewart were very involved in the Hanna Schwalbe Home. Stewart was the chairman and they took a personal interest in the boys who lived there, often inviting them for Shabbat meals. It was on one such occasion that Ronny was heard to say, 'Let's wind up Mrs Lebrett', ... and did. She adored him!

The volunteers were loved by all and they became an important part of our school life. Unfortunately our students did not have many friends outside of school, so the volunteers became their friends and were always eagerly awaited.

Mr Neuberger helps a boy with his tefillin.

It was a treat to have a male volunteer, especially for our boy students. When we began to prepare our boys for bar mitzvah, they were naturally eager to learn to put on *tefillin*[20], so we

---

20. The tefillin is a pair of small boxes which contains parchment on which is written verses from the Bible. These are worn on the arm and head during the morning prayers. One of the highlights of the bar mitzvah is that the boy – now a man – starts

spread the word that we needed male volunteers – and hit the jackpot. Willie Neuberger, for many years president of the Golders Green Beth HaMedrash, offered to come in daily to teach the boys. It was an instant success. No-one looked happier than Mr Neuberger when he attended a bar mitzvah and stood next to a boy he had taught. Both Mr and Mrs Neuberger, their son Michael and their daughter Carmel, our speech therapist, were what I might term great 'Kishronites'. I thank them and all the other good souls who so greatly enhanced the life of our school.

As for the volunteers, they loved coming and often told me how much they appreciated the chance to get to know our students and to realise what exceptional personalities they were, undiminished by their disabilities and, indeed, endowed with a special courage because of them.

The Unsung Heroes

If this book appears to be all about the children and their lives at Kisharon, that is my intention. However, we would never have got off the ground, developed and grown, if not for the executive committee, secretarial staff and, of course, the support of the local Education Office and the Department for Education.

I attended the executive meetings and Mr Bentley, our long-serving chairman, always encouraged me to give a school report. Occasionally a board member visited the school but on the whole they concentrated on fundraising and public relations. Mr Bentley came very often and he and his wife graced all our special events. My husband, Manny, was very active, especially in the beginning, knocking on doors to

---

wearing the tefillin.

collect money needed to get going, and speaking to 'high ups' who would be impressed with his 'professorship'. He never once complained that I was so busy, in fact was happy that we both had absorbing jobs.

At all times we had an educational advisor, some salaried and some who gave of their time and knowledge as a contribution to Kisharon. During the first year I met once a month with Sheila Mortimer who was head of Mapledown Special School. Over a cup of tea we discussed Kisharon's progress and she gave me excellent advice from her extensive experience.

Lillian Chavert was a lecturer at a teacher training college who observed student teachers and knew every special school in London. Almost every week Lillian took me to an interesting school where I could watch teaching in progress and check out equipment. I was often very impressed with the grand building, extensive playground and even a swimming pool. However, I nearly always came back thinking to myself: Yes, we could do with all the things money could buy and yes, one day we will no doubt have them. But, for the moment, our children had what is crucial – loving care in a structured, well thought out programme. When I voiced my thoughts, Lillian could only agree wholeheartedly.

Dorothy Oppenheimer (Op) was very encouraging and supportive. She introduced me to Tavistock Clinic where she was a child psychologist and this proved to be a very useful contact for some of our students. Unfortunately Dorothy passed away, but her kind words and advice helped set the tone of the school in its early days and is in a sense a fitting memorial to her.

Nora Gates was our education advisor. Her regular twice-weekly visits began just before Pesach and, after wandering around to view the school as a whole, she returned to my office with a puzzled expression. 'Chava, I've never seen so many frogs: big frogs, little frogs, green and yellow frogs. Why so much interest in frogs'? I had to laugh as I explained the ten plagues[21] and how Pesach (like all our festivals) was reflected in our daily programme.

As related in a previous chapter, Nora accompanied us to Israel. Her wide knowledge and great sense of humour were of immense benefit to the school in general and to me in particular.

Lena Baum was an expert on play, but her main imprint was to give me sound advice when I felt I was floundering. She taught me to lead from the front and to make decisions with confidence.

There were many more people who helped us along the way, and I end this chapter by thanking everyone who took an interest in Kisharon, and in particular Edith Rothschild, who in 1976 was head of the 'Beis Yaakov School'. The night before Kisharon opened, I suddenly paused. 'What have I done'? I panicked. 'Am I crazy'?

I rang Mrs Rothschild who in her calm way counselled me, 'Do your best and play it by ear'.

As each day was different and each child was different and you could never be sure what would happen next, this

---

21. The Ten Plagues where inflicted on the Egyptians by God when they held the Jews as slaves for 200 years in 1300 BCE. As a result of these plagues, Pharaoh finally sent the Jews free. The second of these plagues was that frogs filled Egypt like flies. Pesach – the Passover – is the annual celebration of the Jewish Exodus from Egypt.

Second minibus from 'Breakaway' and Variety Club.

was the best advice I could be given.

We did our best, the children did their best and, as we loved them and often had to 'play it by ear', we usually hit the right note.

North London Friends Of Kisharon

The story of this amazing group of ladies, with their constant support over the years, could be a whole chapter. Apart from organising the coach and wonderful coach escorts that brought the children from North London, and dealing with all the problems involved in this, they masterminded a fundraising evening once a year that was the highlight of the calendar. Mrs Eva Tunk, Mrs Faigy Levy and the hard-working ladies put together a show year after year – a well-known speaker, a chorus, and the indomitable Mrs Josebacvili, one of our parents whose rousing words moved everyone to tears. The guests sat around beautifully laid tables, enjoying a feast of homemade goodies made by the various ladies of the committee. Low overheads meant that the money raised not only kept the coach on the road, but it also provided the money for the annual holiday to Skeet. The support that this group gave to me went beyond the money they raised. Special tribute must go to all the coach escorts, but particularly Mrs Bennett and Rosalind Solomon who had sole care of a coach load of children during the often long journey to and from Stamford Hill in heavy traffic with often tired and challenging children.

Roll Of Honour

In appreciation of some of the 'backroom boys' who kept the show on the road!

Walter Bentley *	Yuri Curtis
Philip Goldberg	Bernard Goldblum
Ken Gradon *	Stephen Greenman
Michael Katz	Stewart Lebrett
Fred Rosenberg *	Jonathan Schleider
Max Sulbacher	Bernard Trent
Malcolm Wulwick	

* Deceased ז"ל

Part Four
And They Grow Up

Tefillah Lechol Yisrael[1]

Many years ago, I attended a bar mitzvah in the provinces. I was told that the uncle of the bar mitzvah boy had Down's Syndrome and it would be interesting for me to observe an older person with this condition. It was, but for a very different reason than that which the person had in mind.

The uncle, who must have been about 40 years old, stood in the front row. He was obviously ill at ease. His eyes kept

---

1. 'Prayer for everyone'. This section discusses the way a disabled person can participate in the religious community (The *kehilla*). It is important to understand the centrality of the synagogue (shul) and praying (davening) in the life of the Orthodox Jewish community. Jews pray (daven) three times a day. On the Sabbath (Shabbat) this means going to the shul four times. An hour Friday night, two hours on Saturday morning, half an hour in the afternoon and another 15 minutes when Shabbat ends. 'Going to shul' is very much part of the Shabbat atmosphere. Davening is not only a dialogue between Man and God – it is a communal activity. The 'togetherness' of the kehilla is not the outcome of the need to pray together – it is the very root of the act of prayer. In fact prayers that are not said in a quorum of ten Jewish men (a minyan) is considered an inferior level of prayer.

darting around trying to follow what everyone was doing. He clearly had no idea when to sit and when to stand, although he made valiant attempts to do what everyone else was doing. He took his *kippah* off, put it on again and looked anxious and perplexed. Right at the end, with everyone responding to the final *kaddish*[2], the noise must have been the last straw. He took off his *kippah*, rammed it into his pocket and fled from the *shul*.

This is a typical example of one of the many problems facing a disabled person. Understanding and participating in *davening* is difficult for children with learning and concentration difficulties and some may never be able to read a *Sidur*[3] or *Chumash*. Nevertheless, acquiring the knowledge to enable an appropriate level of participation in a community even to enjoy attending *shul* is possible for nearly everyone.

How is this possible? Fortunately, there is a great deal of repetition in our *davening*. Many of our prayers are recited three times a day, seven days a week. A child exposed at an early age to the sound of *davening* will pick up the words, especially if they are sung to well-known melodies. Almost every child, given help and encouragement, can soon recognise when to stand, when to sit, when to respond Amen and when, for example, during the silent prayer to understand that he must be quiet and not disturb anyone.

All this will not happen in a week or a month. It has to be a gradual process suited to the needs and abilities of each child. A great deal will depend on the patience of the parents and the attitude of the community.

A child who finds it difficult to learn to read can still

---

2. Kaddish – the final prayer at the end of the service.
3. The Sidur is a prayer book, the Chumash is the Bible.

learn to pray – *by heart*. One must not wait until reading is established; it many never happen and then time has been wasted. Even if a child *does* learn to read – and hopefully he will – the pace of the prayers in our *shuls* is such that even many adults have a problem keeping up! A child who knows several passages by heart and knows when to say Amen can then attain a level of participation which will help him sit quietly with a picture book during those parts that are too difficult for him.

The inflexible rule is 'Start as you mean to go on'. It may look cute for a three year old to sit on the steps of the *bimah*,[4] but it is definitely not so cute when the child is 10 or 15. Even if kindly congregants see nothing wrong, parents have to set rules for a child from day one.

If he comes to shul, he has to sit still and follow as much as possible. The child should be given a sidur with large print and have an identical sidur at home. If he is given help in turning the pages appropriately, he will eventually begin to recognise the page numbers and find the more familiar prayers himself.

It is best to introduce a child to shul going by taking him towards the end of the prayers when there is usually more singing and then he can leave with everyone else. Obviously all these ideas impose an extra strain on a parent and will almost certainly disrupt his own prayers. However, it is well worth the trouble if, as your child grows up, he (and you) are able to participate more and more. If you start by allowing him to roam the shul when he is a toddler, it will be almost impossible to introduce appropriate behaviour at a later stage.

Education is never easy and unfortunately adults in shul

---

4. A raised central stage in the synagogue from which parts of the service take place.

> **A Letter From A Satisfied Parent –**
> **Originally published in the British Jewish press.**
>
> *Well Done Kisharon*
>
> Sir, – We should like to say a big thank you to Mrs Lehman of the Kisharon Day School and her staff for the hard and sometimes thankless task they have to cope with.
>
> Our daughter has been there three years and she has done very well. She has just come home from a three-day visit to Carmel College.
>
> She is proficient in Hebrew and to hear her read makes us very proud. She is now ready to move on, but, unfortunately, there another problem begins.
>
> We would like her to go to another Jewish school and hope there is one that will accept her, so that she will be able to continue the good start that Kisharon has given her. It's a pity we cannot have any more schools like this.
>
> Congratulations to the head teacher and staff of the Kisharon, and long may they continue.

are not always good role models. It is essential, however, to take your child to a shul where there is reasonable decorum and plenty of singing. It is also important that the Rabbi and congregants are aware of what you are trying to do and willing to assist, not jeopardise, your efforts by misplaced kindness.

But what of the parents in all this? Some children really cannot go to shul and some may not even be able to learn to pray by heart. Parents are used to staying in with young children, but it is not so easy if your son or daughter is perhaps 15 or 20 and cannot go to shul.

There is no simple remedy, but there is light at the end of the tunnel as more and more people in our community learn to accept disability in all its forms as part of our lives. We must increase communal awareness and change our perception of life to accommodate everyone.

Hopefully our new more enlightened way of thinking will be beneficial all round. We have to enable parents of housebound children to go to shul by offering to look after them for an hour. Parents who have similar problems could perhaps get together so that one of them can go to shul and the other can care for both children at home.

Yes, shul must be for all of us. Both adults and children must be given the opportunity to go to shul and given a chance to have their prayers heard – together with the rest of the community.

And The Tears...

We laughed and we cried. Working with the children on a daily basis and for any length of time, one sees only the personalities and not the disabilities. The children had a special charisma and a certain 'canniness'; they knew exactly whom they could play up and who wouldn't put up with any nonsense. One little pupil could throw a terrible 'wobbly' as her mother called it. She was tiny and beautiful with a good vocabulary but, when she got going with her teeth, feet and nails, she could really harm you. Few of our staff could manage her, but

Denah, who is a wonderful teacher, had no difficulty.

'I'm going to have a tantrum', announced the perky six year old.

'Well, go on then', replied Denah in a bored voice. Silence, a glare and a return to the task in hand – and no tantrum!

For her parents, it was all heartbreak. Finally, after she broke a plate glass window, they sent her to residential school where in time the 24-hour programme modified her behaviour and she began to use all her talents. The night before she left us some of our students happened to give a concert. When she sang '*HaMalach HaGoel*' in her beautiful voice, you could have heard a pin drop and, if you listened carefully, quite a few sniffles.

Alan was another child whose 'wobblies' were much worse as he was quite tall, though very thin. The day after he pinned his carer to the floor of the minibus, I was lucky enough to find Ron, a tall, strong teacher who was taking a break from his career as a music therapist in order to study behaviour management. He asked me to give him a room where he and Alan could work.

That room became their first project. They cleaned it, painted it and sewed and hung curtains. Everything was so well-organised that Alan soon found himself writing, doing maths and woodwork and developing many other skills needed to do the job properly. The room began to look really good and Alan was very proud of his work. When at first he threw his usual wobblies, Ron would hold him and say, 'All right, let's calm down and start all over again'. This, plus the fascination he showed in all the projects, seemed to work.

When the room was ready, Ron and Alan baked biscuits and sent handwritten invitations to various children and staff members 'to come for tea'. This was a huge breakthrough for a boy who at first couldn't be taught even in a small group. They then invited us to be measured against a chart on the wall and, once again, Alan was the host in his room, proudly taking all the measurements and entering them on his chart.

Whenever Ron took a much-needed break, Alan loved working on the computer in my office. In the evenings he would ring me and we would always have the same conversation:

'Hello'.
'Hello, Alan. Are you having a good evening'?
'Yes, what are you doing'?
'I'm sitting in my armchair sewing'.
'Then what will you do'?
'Then I'll prepare supper'.
'Then what will you do'?
'I'll eat supper with my family'.
'Then what will you do'?
'I'll clear away'.

... And this would go on until his mother took the phone away from him.

This highlights the plight of children who cannot occupy themselves, have few friends and drive their parents to distraction in the evening and at weekends. Siblings may not want to invite friends to their house and are not always prepared to play with their less able brother or sister. Many tears are shed. Communal awareness of this problem and action would be of great help. Neighbours could take a child for a while or send in older children to help. Organisations which run excellent evening and weekend programmes should be given every possible help, both practical and monetary, so that they can concentrate on the children and not waste time agonising over finance.

Naturally, in some cases, parents have asked me about the possibility of marriage for their child. In all the years I worked in Kisharon, I never found a satisfactory answer. There have been a few marriages, some have worked and others have not. At all these weddings I rejoiced with the parents as we cried with happiness. Even if one did not work out well, I was still glad that the couple involved had had their own special time. They had experienced the excitement of being a *chatan* and *kallah*[5]; they had enjoyed all the preparations and attention of family and friends. For once in their lives, they too had danced with their friends at the very centre of the circle! So it hadn't worked, but it might have and, in the meantime, they had tasted life as it could be, not viewing it tearfully from the edge of the circle.

---

5. Bride and bridegroom (actually the other way round – in Hebrew the groom is mentioned first).

Acknowledgments

I regret that I did not keep a diary and I hope that I will be forgiven if I missed out mentioning people who were closely involved with Kisharon. They know who they are and they know how much I appreciated everyone who was part of the team.

I have especially fond memories of all those boys and girls who came with us on holiday, cooked for us and generally made our holidays special in their company.

I would like to thank Renee Vorhaus and Chaya Raphael who edited the text and twitched it into shape.

I am grateful to our sons Benny Yonatan and Rafi who worked hard getting this book published as well as supporting us in so many ways.

Thank you Yonatan for helping to turn the manuscript into a book and dealing with all the details for which I had no patience!

I thank my dear husband Manny, who never minded my total commitment to Kisharon and always encouraged me. Though Machla and Esti, our daughters, live in America, their phone calls, emails and visits give support and make them feel not so far away.

Special thanks go to my patient, kind, and caring publisher Chaim Mazo, who also designed the front cover, which is based on a drawing by our granddaughter Yam.